RENOVATING A
KITCHEN

FROM THE EDITORS OF **Fine Homebuilding**®

The Taunton Press

The Taunton Press
Inspiration for hands-on living®

The Taunton Press, Inc., 63 South Main Street, PO Box 5506, Newtown, CT 06470-5506
e-mail: tp@taunton.com

COVER AND INTERIOR DESIGN: Cathy Cassidy
LAYOUT: Suzie Yannes
FRONT COVER PHOTOGRAPHER: Roe A. Osborn
BACK COVER PHOTOGRAPHERS: Rich Ziegner, courtesy *Fine Homebuilding*, © The Taunton Press, Inc. (top left and bottom right), Scott Gibson, courtesy *Fine Homebuilding*, © The Taunton Press, Inc. (top right), Bruce Greenlaw, courtesy *Fine Homebuilding*, © The Taunton Press, Inc. (bottom left)

For Pros by Pros® is a trademark of The Taunton Press, Inc., registered in the U.S. Patent and Trademark Office

Library of Congress Cataloging-in-Publication Data

Renovating a kitchen / from the editors of Fine homebuilding.
     p. cm. — (For pros, by pros)
  ISBN 1-56158-540-8
  1. Kitchens—Remodeling. I. Fine homebuilding. II. Series.
TH4816.3.K58 R453 2002
643'.4—dc21
                         2002151273

Printed in the United States of America
10 9 8 7 6 5 4

The following manufacturers/names appearing in *Renovating a Kitchen* are trademarks: Sub-Zero, Johnson Industries, General Electric, Maytag, Gaggenau, Polyseamseal, Wasser High-Tech Coatings, Custom Building Products, Dens-Shield, Georgia-Pacific, Fine Homebuilding, Tile Council of America, Makita, DuPont, Corian, Avonite, Surell, Gibralter, Golden Eagle, Lexan, Scotch-Brite, Avonite, Dupont, Fountainhead, International Paper, Formica, IKEA, Blum, Alfit, Amerock, Mepla, Salice, KraftMaid, Rutt, Kitchen Cabinet and Manufacturers Association, Merillat, Home Depot, National Kitchen and Bath Association, Conestoga, Thermofoil, Excalibur, Biesemeyer, Hydrocote, Freud, Hafele, Rev-A-Shelf, Rockwell, Viking, Broan, KitchenAid, Star Wars, Star Trek, Home Mechanix, The Home Ventilation Institute, Cabinet Factory, The American Society of Heating, Refrigerating and Air-Conditioning Engineers' Standard 62, Ben & Jerry's.

Special thanks to the authors, editors, art directors,

copy editors, and other staff members of *Fine Homebuilding*

who contributed to the development of the articles in this book.

CONTENTS

PART 3: PLANNING A KITCHEN REMODEL

INTRODUCTION

The most important fixture in my mom's kitchen was never the stove, or the refrigerator, or even the sink. It was a stool. Early in my life it was a metal stool, yellow and chrome, with fold-out steps. Then later it was a wooden stool that I screwed together out of two-by-fours with a big maple cutting board for a seat. That stool was where my mother sat to drink her instant coffee, smoke her cigarettes, and write her grocery lists. It's where guests perched to acclimate themselves to our home. And it's where I sat after dinner to avoid doing my homework.

If my mother were remodeling her kitchen today, I know she would start with the stool. But kitchens are highly personal spaces, and other people would start with the restaurant range they've always wanted or the farmhouse sink. Eventually, though, everybody gets around to the functional heart of the kitchen: cabinets and countertops. Whatever else a kitchen might be—sanctuary, gathering place, status symbol—it is first and foremost a culinary workshop where food is stored and prepared. Try doing that without cabinets and counters.

In this book, which is a collection of articles originally published in *Fine Homebuilding* ® magazine, you'll find practical advice about building, choosing, and installing the essential elements of a kitchen. Well, most of them anyway; there's nothing here about stools.

—Kevin Ireton,
editor-in-chief, *Fine Homebuilding*

Kitchen Cabinets from Components

■ BY JOEL WHEELER AND SVEN HANSON

For more than 13 years we've been building premium furniture and custom cabinets in Albuquerque, N.M. In that time, costs have risen, but competition has kept our prices low. About five years ago, we began looking for a partner who could help us stay competitive. That partner turned out to be not just one but a group of companies that make cabinet components.

Component manufacturers make everything from a single, simple square box to elaborate assemblies that will cover the wall. The cabinets arrive in tightly packaged bundles of flat panels (called knocked down, or KD). Large retailers such as IKEA℠ sell KD cabinets to brave and thrifty do-it-yourselfers. The retailers include extensive instructions with the components, and market them under the category RTA, which means ready-to-assemble. We often get calls from do-it-yourselfers to help them

Wood adds the custom touch. This bright, Santa Fe-style kitchen is dressed up with cabinet doors and drawer fronts made of pickled maple. The cabinets behind them are affordable modular boxes made of laminated particleboard.

to complete their jobs, so we don't mind the competition.

Some fabricators deal in machined components made of particleboard veneered with vinyl, polyester, or wood. Others carry solid-wood components such as face frames, boxes, doors, drawer fronts, shelves, and drawer sides and bottoms.

Manufacturers show their wares in well-organized catalogs. For some (Components Plus), you specify what you want, and they tell you what you need and give you the prices. Others (Cab-Parts) let you pick from a huge assortment of shapes and sizes. Then, you add up the costs based on the price list and order the parts by catalog designation.

Typically, we buy KD cabinets and drawers from one manufacturer, doors from another and hardware from our local mail-order distributor TJ Hardware Inc. If we need a hardwood drawer, we go to another fabricator. The result is a set of cabinets that combine the look of custom woodwork with the efficiency of modular construction (photo, facing page). As a ballpark price, you can figure the base cabinets will cost about $70 per running ft. and the upper cabinets $60 per ft. This price includes the carcases, drawers, raised-panel doors, and necessary

Hardware first. Before assembling the boxes, Michael Fratrick screws the hinges and the drawer tracks to the sides of the cabinet. The holes to the left of the slide receive the doweled drawer divider.

worked to standardize all aspects of cabinet dimension and construction. That standardization included ditching traditional face-frame cabinets in favor of slab construction.

The hinge hides on the backside of the door, and the flanges that secure the hinge to the cabinet have screw holes on 32-mm centers. The doors hide all but about ⅛ in. of the edge of the carcase. The universal nature of the door-to-hinge-to-cabinet relationship permits a complete remodel of the cabinets for the cost of a new set of doors and the time it takes to install them. For cabinetmakers, that's a good way to sell around the "I'm not sure I'll like it forever" objection.

By ordering premachined parts, we run a safer, cleaner, quieter shop. Each job ties up the shop floor for less than half the time that it takes to build cabinets from scratch. But you've got to knock them together fast. Even more importantly, you must take the basics of a floor plan, turn it into a functioning design and, from it, order the correct parts.

> *For a kitchen to look right, the majority of the doors need to be taller than they are wide.*

hardware. All these parts fit together because the dimensions are standardized and we are meticulous in our specifications.

They Call It Eurostyle

Component makers offer the greatest cost savings when supplying frameless cabinets predrilled with two vertical rows of holes spaced on 32-mm centers (photo, above). These holes, about 1¼ in. apart, accept shelf pins and hardware-mounting screws.

This style of cabinet construction is called Eurostyle because it was developed in Europe as a response to the devastation of World War II. Europeans needed to get back into the 20th century quickly, and they had to do the job with limited resources. Fractured forests yielded more particleboard than solid lumber, and a decimated work force didn't have time to rebuild an entire continent using their traditional hand craftsmanship. So cabinetmakers and manufacturers of machinery and hardware

Ordering the Cabinets

We begin the cabinet layout with a plan of the room and place center lines on counter-mounted fixtures such as sinks and range tops. Then, we draw in boundaries for areas reserved for stove, refrigerator, compactor, dishwasher, and microwave (consult the appliance manuals for clearance requirements). We're also careful to note the positions of walls, doorways, and windows on the plan.

From these fixed positions, we determine the unbroken runs of cabinets and figure out how many it will take to fill out the run. Cabinets are sized in 1½-in. or 3-in. increments, depending on which company we're ordering from. Any gaps left over are finished with filler strips.

We prefer to keep cabinet doors in the range of 20-in. wide. Doors that are wider than 22 in. to 24 in. have a tendency to warp, and their manufacturers won't guarantee them for flatness. For a kitchen to look right, the majority of the doors need to be taller than they are wide.

We can order cabinets that have non-stock dimensions, but there's a hefty penalty to pay. A typical premium is $5 to $10 for a change in width or depth, and $15 for a change in height. And if you've got a base cabinet with nonstandard drawers, you can figure an additional charge of about $3 per drawer. So when the dimensions get odd, the costs mount quickly. Ideally, the doors of the upper cabinets should line up with doors and drawers of the lower cabinets. In practice, however, this is tough to accomplish. Windows, sinks, and other obstacles often derail the strictly aligned approach.

At inside corners it's important to use adequate filler strips (at least 2 in. wide) to allow drawers and doors on both sides of the corner to pass each other. Clients can more easily forgive oversize fillers than cabinet doors that can't be opened. We also want fillers at wall intersections to allow us to scribe to the curvy walls typical of New Mexico's residential architecture. In Eurostyle, we don't have an overhanging face frame to provide scribing room.

Basic dimensions figured, we go to the appropriate catalog—or, in the case of Components Plus, we just fax them our list of sizes, and they fax us back our list and the prices. One way or the other, the business of estimating a cabinet installation is greatly simplified by having the first half of our cost computed exactly. The Components Plus order can even include the hardware, and that might sway a first-timer or a builder working in a remote location. But you'll save more money by buying in bulk (25 slides or 50 hinges) from a hardware supplier.

Quick Assembly Is the Key

We win or lose the time/money part of this deal at the assembly stage, so we set up the shop to allow our best mechanics to work at full speed. When the parts arrive, we put them into groups: drawer sides; individual cabinet sides and tops; backs; and miscellaneous parts. After this step, we drive the dowels into the horizontal members—cabinet bottoms and drawer dividers. The dowels are held fast by a glue supplied by the manufacturer.

Our cabinet assemblers work on a smooth, 18-in. high bench, assembling the boxes according to a set of instructions provided by the manufacturer. With two cabinet sides laid flat and placed top to top, mechanic Michael Fratrick lightly pencils in positions for hardware. Fratrick uses the Magic Wand, a layout tool made by Blum®. If you don't have one of these tools, you can use a good ruler with enhanced markings to show the 32-mm centers and the positions of the hinges and drawer slides.

On a base cabinet, Michael positions the drawer slides and hinge mounting plates (photo, facing page). He fastens them into the holes with 5mm stud screws. He then squirts a bit of glue into each of the dowel holes on one cabinet side and wrestles the horizontal parts into proper position. He drives them down by striking the dowels on the other end with a rubber hammer.

The back goes in next, then the other side goes on (top photo, p. 8), and the rubber hammer slams it home. Instead of clamping, we staple the joint, which provides additional reinforcement.

Michael places the cabinet face down and squares it up by comparing diagonal measurements. Meanwhile, our other mechanic, Karen Umland, glues the hanger bar (a strip of plywood that reinforces the cabinet back where the mounting screws will attach it to the wall) along the top edge by pressing it into a wavy bead of hot glue. With the same hot glue, she puts a bead, or fillet, around the back-panel perimeter (center photo, p. 8). The result: a square, sturdy cabinet. We have never gotten a customer complaint on carcase quality.

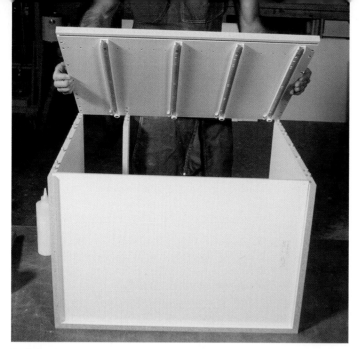

Building a box. Hardware installed, the box is ready to assemble. Here, the last side is aligned with dowels in the top, the bottom, and the drawer divider. The back panel will tuck into the dado in the cabinet side.

Glue secures the back panel. Karen Umland runs a bead of hot glue around the back panel to affix it to the cabinet's sides, back, and bottom. The plywood strip on the right is a hanger bar for the cabinet.

Drawers are just small cabinets. Also made of laminate-covered particleboard, the drawer boxes have the same construction details as their cabinets. Here, a drawer slide is being affixed to the bottom of the drawer.

Next, the Drawers

The drawers go together in the same manner as the cabinet carcases. It may seem like a small thing, but the repetitive process means we don't have to change tools or mental gears. No doubt the similarity of material and structure saves time at the factory, too.

After sliding the bottom into place, Michael hammers on the other side. Then, he checks the drawer for square and runs a bead of hot glue around the bottom-to-side connection. He next installs the tracks with ⅝-in. #6 nickel-plate deep-thread screws (bottom photo).

Ordering and Drilling the Doors

The doors make up the vast majority of visible surface on a true Eurostyle-cabinet job, so we put a lot of energy into helping the client choose the doors. Ordering doors is simplest when done through your carcase suppliers. They'll automatically make the doors to fit, but you're usually limited to particleboard and laminated work, albeit with some fancy styling including rolled edges and running edge pulls. For a more traditional look, we order raised-panel doors from another source.

Various manufacturers offer a wide selection of wooden doors. Most species are familiar North American hardwoods, but some you may never have heard of. Door manufacturers also offer scores of panel profiles, edge profiles and inside edge-bead profiles. Some suppliers will finish doors for you, and they also will drill for hinges and pulls.

The usual dimensions are the same height as the case, but ⅛ in. (3mm) shorter and narrower. That leaves an ⅛-in. reveal between doors in a run of cabinets. We leave a minimum ³⁄₁₆-in. gap at a wall to ensure room for the door to open.

Our doors arrive without the holes drilled for mounting the hinges. That way, the door suppliers haven't had to concern themselves with which way the doors open, which cuts down on costly mistakes. Now comes the part where the assembler displays some true craftsmanship, or at least a talent for accurate measurement.

The European-style hinge needs three holes to attach to the door (top photo). In the center is a 35mm (1⅜-in.) by 13mm deep hole that receives the hinge cup. The edge of this hole is 2mm to 3mm from the edge of the door. In addition to the 35mm hole, the hinge needs two ⁷⁄₆₄-in. dia. holes for the #6 mounting screws.

We do our drilling with a three-spindle machine costing roughly $2,600 and made by Blum (center photo). Other hinge suppliers offer a similar device.

To mount hinges using an ordinary drill press, you first install the 35mm bit, rotate one cutter next to the fence and move the fence ⅛ in. away from the bit (check the specs for your hinge). Clamp the fence in place. We adjust the table to hold the work 1 in. below the bit and set the depth stop to drill to a depth of ½ in. + ¹⁄₃₂ in. That gives us a little allowance if we have thin stock or dust in the hole.

For the majority of the doors, the center of the 35mm hole is 3³⁄₁₆ in. to 3¾ in. from the top and bottom of the door. So we set the appropriate stops on the drill-press table to let us quickly register the hinge positions. Special-purpose cabinets sometimes need different hinge positions, and tall doors will need additional hinges. A glance at the positions of the hinge-mounting plates on the cabinets tells us whether we are using the correct set of stops on our hinge machine.

To test the accuracy of our stops, we drill hinge-mounting holes in a 2-in.-wide scrap cut to the length of the door. Then, we screw the hinges on the test stick and install the stick on the cabinet. If it sits right and

Hinges are adjustable. Slots in the hinge-mounting plates allow the hinge to be moved in and out, and up and down, which makes it easy to get the door to lay flat, square, and centered on the cabinet.

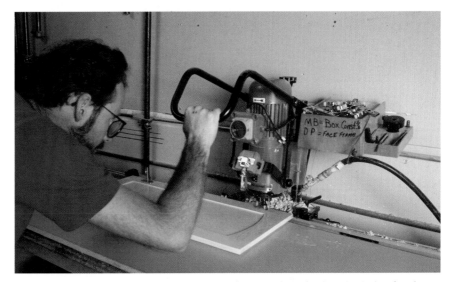

This machine drills three holes at once. When it's done boring the holes for the hinge, this specialized drill press inserts the hinge into the circular mortise.

Installing the doors. Once the boxes are assembled, Fratrick snaps the doors onto their hinges and tinkers with their final positioning with a screwdriver. Sink bases make up the top tier of cabinets. They sit atop a row of base cabinets.

opens cleanly, not hitting cabinet edge or adjacent door, we know the setup is accurate, and we go ahead and drill and attach the doors (bottom photo, p. 9).

Cabinet Ends and Drawer Fronts

Picture the classic window over the sink. Now, glance to the side at the upper cabinets, and you'll likely see a surface that the neophyte designer forgets about. Without some additional treatment, the cabinet sides are probably gleaming white or champagne polyester.

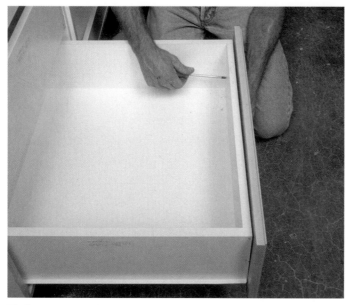

Fitting a drawer front. Drawer fronts in a European-style kitchen must be installed accurately. Two threaded, adjustable inserts are let into 20mm holes in the back of a drawer front (top), which is then attached to the box with machine screws run into the inserts (bottom).

An attractive alternative includes peel-and-stick veneer, prefinished to match the doors and applied to a clean flat end panel. For a slight additional cost, we apply a raised panel to those ends. To make this look right you've got to make sure the visible edge of the panel is finished, and the door has to be wider by the thickness of the panel's frame. The hinge position has to be adjusted accordingly by using a different base plate.

Drawer fronts are the same widths as the doors. Two typical heights for drawer fronts are 5 in. and 6 in. Aligning drawer fronts so that the gaps between adjacent drawers are equal is a finicky business. Back in the old days, we used to rely on tricks such as putting small tabs of double-sided mirror tape on the drawer box. Then, we'd slide the drawer into its box, position the drawer front so that it looked right and press the drawer front to the box, hoping it would stick long enough to anchor it with a couple of screws driven from inside the drawer. Now, we use "drawer-front adjusters" to attach fronts to boxes. The adjuster has a threaded-steel insert floating inside a slot in a 20mm barbed-plastic dowel (top photo, left).

We put one of the adjusters at each end of the drawer front—about 3 in. from the end and roughly centered. The adjusters nest in 20mm holes that are 10.5mm deep. We drop 20mm dowel centers into the holes, press the drawer front to the drawer box and slam it with a fist to mark the drawer box. Through these marks, we drill 5mm holes using a brad-point bit and a backer block to reduce tearout in the drawer.

Then, we press the adjusters into the holes in the drawer front and attach it to the drawer box with a couple of machine screws (bottom photo, left). The inserts in the adjusters allow the drawer front to be moved up and down, and side to side about ⅛ in. in all directions. Once we complete final on-site adjustments, we affix the drawer fronts with a couple of 1¼-in. dry-wall screws (photo, right).

Installation Notes

In a true Eurostyle job, the upper cabinets hang from a metal Z-bar attached to the wall. Installers hang and adjust the cabinets using special cam-action hangers inside the boxes. The hanger-bar system lets a single worker hang cabinets. I suppose these are clever devices, but we don't mess with them. The hardware costs extra, and the cabinets inevitably have to be notched in places to fit over the bars.

Instead, we install the upper cabinets by screwing through the hanger bars that we've glued to the backs of the cabinets. One in-staller holds the bottom aligned with a line drawn level from a point 54 in. above the floor, while the other shoots in the screws. That's American style.

Most of the manufacturers sell a combi-nation leg and leveler for their base cabinets. You adjust the levelers with a screwdriver passed through a small access hole inside the cabinet. A press-on cover then hides the hole. After leveling cabinets, you snap the toe kick onto the front leg levelers.

For a couple of reasons, leg levelers have not received wide acceptance in the United States. In Europe, cabinets typically belong to the household, not to the house. Far fewer Europeans own their own homes than Amer-icans, and when Europeans move, they take their cabinets.

The levelers cost only about $8 per set, but with labor added, that's too much for single use. We construct 4-in.-tall bases of ¾-in. CDX plywood. To level the bases, we crawl the floor with a 4-ft. level until we've determined the highest point in the runs. We start there and level all the bases to that point using shims, construction adhesive, and 2x4 blocks glued and nailed to the floor and screwed to the bases. This makes our foundation strong.

Affixing the drawer front. The adjustable inserts allow the drawer front to be moved ⅛ in. in each direction. When align-ment is right, drywall screws make the positioning permanent.

We still build cabinets from scratch when they have to be customized to fit a particular installation. But for the straightforward jobs, using components effectively doubles the size of our shop and lets our skilled cabinet-makers concentrate on the one-of-a-kind projects that they relish.

We can't claim that cabinets from com-ponents will turn you into a master cabinet-maker. And we can assure you that making cabinets from components won't work if you like to fake it as you do a job. But if you understand the basics of cabinet design and if you can measure accurately and assemble in an orderly fashion, making cabinets from components can really work.

Joel Wheeler is a furniture and cabinet maker in New Mexico.
Sven Hanson ran a woodworking shop in New Mexico for 25 years. Now living in Italy and France, he takes new paths as they present themselves.

Cabinet-component suppliers

The manufacturers listed below offer a range of cabinet components, from KD (knock down) cabinet carcases to hardwood frame-and-panel doors. In addition to these suppliers, which all ship nationwide, there are countless other regional or local shops too small or too busy to advertise nationally.

Accent Manufacturing
105 Leavesly Rd.
Building 3-D
Gilroy, CA 95020
(408) 846-9993
www.accentmfg.com
Cabinet-box components, shelves, drawers, hardware, drilled doors in laminates with custom radii, wood-slab, and veneer doors. Sell to cabinet shops, builders, and related trades.

Cab Parts
716 Arrowest Rd.
Grand Junction, CO 81505
(970) 241-7682
www.cabparts.com
Component cabinets including drawers, adjustable shelves, roll-out drawer boxes. Simple line of cabinets with comprehensive catalog of sizes and styles. Sell to cabinetmakers and contractors who make their own cabinets only.

Components Plus-Vass Inc.
3405 Walnut St.
Denver, CO 80205
(303) 292-1040
Line of melamine cabinet components featuring 1½-in. width increments. Dowels are preinstalled in horizontal pieces. Doors and drawers are predrilled for European hardware. Edge banding available in pvc, laminate, wood tape, or solid wood up to 12 mm thick. Sell to cabinetmakers and contractors who make their own cabinets.

Conestoga Wood Specialties Inc.
245 Reading Rd.
P.O. Box 158
East Earl, PA 17519-0158
(717) 445-3248
www.conestogawood.com
Comprehensive line of frameless and face-frame cabinets, doors, drawers including dovetailed wood. Mind-boggling list of merchandise. Sell to cabinetmakers and manufacturers only.

Hutchinson Products Co.
P.O. Box 12066
Oklahoma City, OK 73157
(800) 847-0091
Wood or MDF door and drawer fronts in slab or frame-and-panel. No finishing, drilling or hardware.

Mar-Flo Inc.
93 Harrison St.
Paterson, NJ 07501
(973) 742-4765
Solid wood doors in more than 100 styles, finished or unfinished. Sell to cabinetmakers, contractors, and savvy owner-builders.

Porta Door
65 Cogwheel Ln.
Seymour, CT 06483
(203) 888-6191
www.portadoor.com
Doors, drawer fronts, and drawer boxes. Finishing available. Sell to cabinetmakers and contractors.

Scherr's Cabinets
5315 Burdick Expy East
Rt. 5, Box #12
Minot, ND 58701
(701) 839-3384
www.scherrs.com
Box components, drawers (including dovetailed solid wood) hardwood doors, raw or stained and finished. Drilling and hardware optional. Sell to cabinet makers, contractors, and savvy owner builders.

Top Drawer Components Inc.
5154 S. Delaware Dr.
Apache Junctions, AZ 85220
(800) 745-9540
www.topdrwr.com
Dovetailed drawers of wood and melamine in sizes from 2-in. to 14-in. high. Assembled or RTA, the wood is finished with two coats of vinyl sealer and one coat of precatalyzed lacquer. Sell to anyone.

Cabinet-hardware suppliers

European-style cabinets require hinges, drawer slides, fasteners, and assorted jigs and tools that aren't always readily available. Here's a list of manufacturers who can steer you to a local supplier, or to mail-order houses that can fill your order.

Amerock® Corp.
4000 Auburn St.
P. O. Box 7018
Rockford, IL 61125-7018
(815) 969-6308
www.amerock.com
USA-made European and traditional hardware.

Julius Blum Inc.
7733 Old Plank Rd.
Stanley, NC 28164
(800) 438-6788
www.blum.com
European hardware, jigs, and tools.

Grass America Inc.
1202 Highway 66 South
Kernersville, NC 27284
(910) 996-4041
www.grassusa.com.
Full range of hinges and hardware.

Mepla-Alfit Inc.
P.O. Box 1666
Lexington, NC 27260
(800) 858-4957
www.mepla-alfit.com
Full range of European hardware, tools and jigs.

Salice America Inc.
2123 Crown Center Dr.
Charlotte, NC 28227
(704) 841-7810
www.saliceamerica.com
Full range of European hinges.

Hybrid Cabinet Construction

■ BY JIM TOLPIN

By now, most Americans know what a typical European kitchen looks like: unadorned, monochrome surfaces separated by crisp joint lines. Besides the streamlined appearance, European-style cabinets are also noted for their accessibility and ease of cleaning. Nevertheless, the Kitchen Cabinet Manufacturers Association[SM] reports that the market share of plastic-laminate doors, characteristic of European-style cabinets, plummeted from 30% in 1980 to 19% in 1990.

To a woodworker like me who makes his best money building European-style kitchen cabinets, this was troubling news. I've found

Through the adroit use of applied moldings, frame-and-panel doors, and applied, beaded-plywood panels, the author created 32mm cabinets with a country-American flavor.

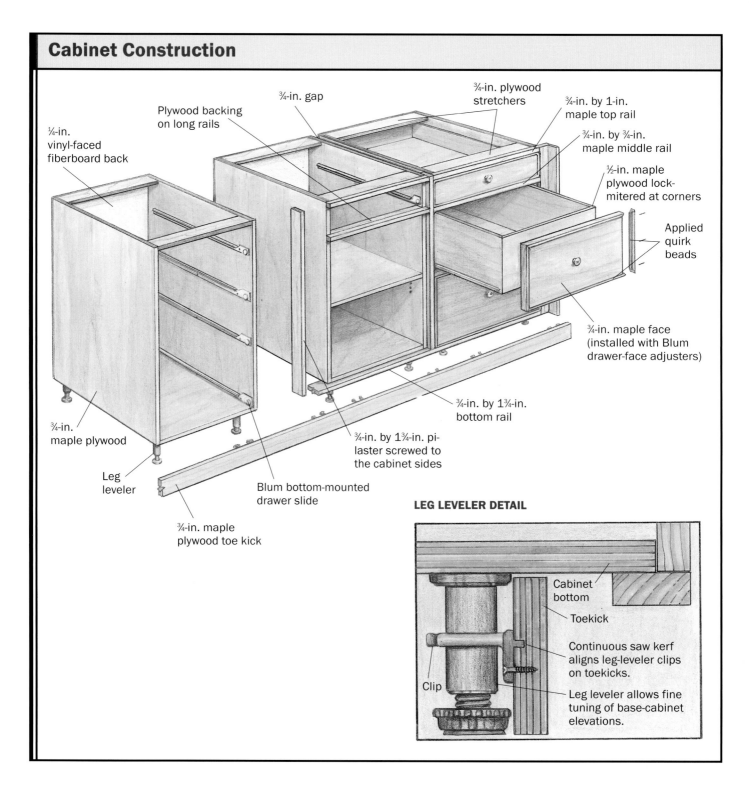

¼-in. gap

Plywood backing on long rails

¼-in. vinyl-faced fiberboard back

¾-in. plywood stretchers

¾-in. by 1-in. maple top rail

¾-in. by ¾-in. maple middle rail

½-in. maple plywood lock-mitered at corners

Applied quirk beads

¾-in. maple face (installed with Blum drawer-face adjusters)

¾-in. maple plywood

Leg leveler

¾-in. by 1¾-in. bottom rail

¾-in. by 1¾-in. pilaster screwed to the cabinet sides

Blum bottom-mounted drawer slide

¾-in. maple plywood toe kick

LEG LEVELER DETAIL

Cabinet bottom

Toekick

Continuous saw kerf aligns leg-leveler clips on toekicks.

Clip

Leg leveler allows fine tuning of base-cabinet elevations.

these cabinets to be incredibly cost effective to build, even in my one-man shop. They have no face frames to make and install; no complex case joints to execute; and no surface-mounted, nonadjustable hinges or sloppy drawer slides to fight with. Instead, modular cases, prefitted with hardware, are assembled quickly and easily using removable fasteners. The hardware, designed specifically for the European 32mm system of cabinetmaking, not only offers ease of installation but also allows the fit of doors and drawers to be fine-tuned without removing and rehanging the components.

Glass and Lead

Before installing the glass door panels, I applied a grid of a self-adhering, bronze-colored lead strip to the face of each panel to create the illusion of divided lights. This product, which is available in various colors, was installed by peeling protective paper off the back to expose an adhesive, then pressing the strip in place with a small rubber roller. I drew reference lines on a piece of cardboard and placed it un-

der the glass to help me align the strips before pressing them in place. Where strips overlapped, I used a small plastic tool (supplied with the came) to mash them together to mimic a solder joint.

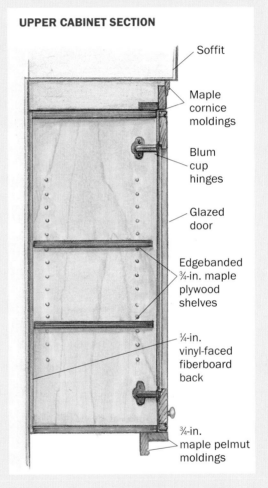

UPPER CABINET SECTION

- Soffit
- Maple cornice moldings
- Blum cup hinges
- Glazed door
- Edgebanded ¾-in. maple plywood shelves
- ¼-in. vinyl-faced fiberboard back
- ¾-in. maple pelmut moldings

When Mark and Martha Ditchfield asked me to build them a "country" kitchen to complete their kitchen remodel, I decided it was time to apply the 32mm system to the creation of traditional, "American-style" cabinets. This would allow me to use all the nifty specialty tools and jigs (not to mention the know-how) that I had acquired over the past few years. The challenge would be to create the look of face-frame cabinets with

applied moldings and end panels that would work with the 32mm system.

Design by Mail

In preparation for new cabinets, the Ditchfields had gutted their old kitchen and pantry. I drafted two copies of the kitchen's floor plan at a scale of 1 in. to 1 ft., then sketched plan views of the upper cabinets on one copy and the base cabinets on the other. I located the stove, the refrigerator, the dishwasher, and the pantry first, then filled in the blanks with cabinets. Not including the pantry unit, lengths of individual carcases would range from 18 in. for a stack of drawers to 43½ in. for the corner units, well within my tolerances (for ease of handling, I never build cabinet sections longer than 60 in.).

Country-Style Modules

The Ditchfields wanted their cabinets to be built of a light-colored wood with a natural finish, so I chose maple as the primary material. The maple would be lacquered to allow the grain and the color to show through.

Conforming to the 32mm system, the basic carcases would consist of edgebanded, seven-ply, ¾-in. A-3 ("A" grade on the face; "3" grade on the back) maple plywood tops, bottoms and sides (plywood stretchers for the tops of the base units), butt-joined with knockdown (removable) fasteners and backed with ¼-in. white-vinyl faced fiberboard (drawing, p. 14). I use knockdown fasteners because they're easy to install, strong enough to eliminate the need for rabbets and dadoes and can be quickly removed should the cabinets need to be dismantled and modified on the job site. Instead of displaying the plastic-laminate surfaces usually associated with 32mm cabinets, the visible sides and backs of the base units would be faced with ¼-in. kadama "Beaded Victoria Panels" from States Industries. Kadama is an Indonesian hardwood that complements maple in grain and color. Also available in red oak, the panels are commonly used for wainscoting. The exposed ends of the upper cabinets would be faced with plain ¾-in. A-3 maple plywood panels.

The Ditchfield's cabinets would also feature frame-and-panel doors: solid Eastern hard-maple frames surrounding either ¼-in. beaded kadama panels or double-strength glass panels embellished with applied lead came (sidebar, p. 15). Drawers would have ½-in. maple plywood fronts, backs, and sides fitted with ¼-in. maple plywood bottoms, and solid-maple faces. All doorframes and drawer faces would be outlined by an applied quirk bead. An easy-to-install detail, the applied bead would reinforce the kitchen's country appearance.

Typical of 32mm cabinets, the doors and the drawer faces would overlay the front edges of the carcases, concealing the edges when closed. However, instead of butting end-to-end in the usual manner, the carcases would be spaced ¾ in. apart, with the resulting gaps concealed by solid maple pilasters. Pilasters would also be installed between the three sets of double doors, next to the appliances and at the inside corners of the cabinets. Finally, horizontal top, bottom, and middle rails would be nailed to the base cabinets, flush with the pilasters.

The resulting facades would give the appearance of doors and drawer faces flush-mounted in conventional face frames (photo, p. 13). Applied cornice and pelmut moldings, a tiled countertop, and ceramic pulls would complete the country-American motif.

This hybrid design would allow the use of 32mm-system hardware throughout: concealed adjustable door hinges, bottom-mounted drawer slides, 5mm brass shelf clips and, finally, adjustable legs for the base units covered by removable plywood toe-kicks. Amenities would include two space-conserving, half-moon lazy Susans and a countertop appliance garage enclosed by a shop-built tambour door.

Carcase Cutting

Once the Ditchfields approved my plan, the next step was to develop cutlists for all the cabinet parts. I began by listing on a chart all the components specific to each unit. From this chart, it was easy to develop specific cutlists for the components in each category.

Additional charts listed the moldings and the applied panels. I used these charts to develop master cutlists. One list specified the total lineal footage of solid stock that would be required in specific widths. A second list of plywood components was converted to graphic illustrations of 4-ft. by 8-ft. panels layed out for optimal yield.

Armed with this information, I started cutting parts out of a forbiddingly tall stack of plywood. I cut most panels on a table saw fitted with an Excalibur® rip fence and extension table. Parts that were too narrow to crosscut safely against the fence (anything less than 14 in. wide) were crosscut on a radial-arm saw equipped with a Biesemeyer® sliding stop, carefully indexed to match the indicator on the table-saw fence. Accurate to within 1/64 in., the rip fence and the sliding stop are easy to adjust and eliminate the need for constant checking with a tape measure.

With the panels cut, I hauled all the parts targeted for edgebanding to a production cabinet shop equipped with an expensive, but fast and reliable, edgebanding machine. Edgebanding can be done with a variety of hand-held machines, but I've found them to be excruciatingly slow when working with a large volume of stock. This edgebanding job cost about $100.

Drilling the Cases

With the stock edgebanded and back in the shop, I drilled ⅜-in. holes in the bottom panels of the base units to receive standard Blum nylon "leg levelers." Next, I drilled a series of 5mm holes in the side panels to provide attachment points for shelf clips, hinge plates, and drawer slides.

This operation was accomplished easily with the use of a drilling jig designed specifically for 32mm construction (photo, above). Made by J and R Enterprises, Inc., the jig has two graduated steel fences (one that bears against the top edge of the panel and the other against the bottom edge)

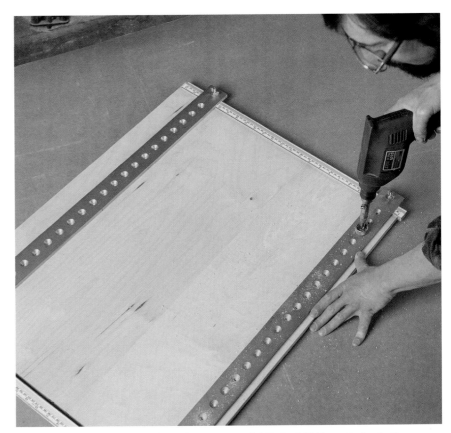

Tolpin used his portable drill and a commercial jig to drill 5mm holes in the carcase sides for attaching hinge plates, drawer slides, and shelf clips.

linked by two brass-colored aluminum drilling templates that rest on the face of the panel. The templates locate the front and rear rows of holes on the 32mm grid, which is essential when drilling for drawer slides and adjustable shelf clips. This jig, which sells for $190, comes with a 5mm brad-point drill bit fitted with an adjustable depth-stop centering collar.

For custom cabinetmakers, there's no need to drill all the holes on the 32mm grid. That's why I use a device called "The Magic Wand" with my drilling jig. It's a 1m-long, clear plastic scale (marked in inches and millimeters) with 5mm dia. holes on 32mm centers, the same as the drilling jig. A variety of plastic inserts snap into these holes to represent hinge plates, drawer slides, shelf clips, and other hardware, which allow me to mock up any hardware configuration. The bad news is that this product (once sold by Blum) is no longer manufactured,

After sanding all the cabinet parts with 180-grit sandpaper, I lacquered everything except the drawers and the doors, which would be finished after assembly. Interior surfaces received a coat of sanding sealer followed by two coats of gloss lacquer, while exterior surfaces (and later, the doors and the drawers) received a coat of sealer plus three coats of semigloss lacquer. I used Hydrocote® finishing products; they're nontoxic, nonflammable, fast-drying, and cure to a clear, durable, water-resistant finish. Each coat was sanded with 220-grit wet/dry sandpaper, and the final coat was buffed with 400-grit wet/dry sandpaper.

Doors and Drawers

Before assembling the carcases (which would quickly eat up limited shop space), I tackled the doors and the drawers. Using a ¼-in. slotting cutter and a router table, I cut a groove in the edge of each stile and rail for the kadama panels. The grooves stop short of the stile ends, so they don't show at the tops and the bottoms of the doors. I assembled the doorframes using biscuits and yellow glue, cutting the slots for the biscuits on a stationary biscuit joiner. Because plywood panels are dimensionally stable, I glued the panels into their grooves.

After glue-up, I used a router to round over the doorframes around the panel perimeters and to rabbet the back sides of the nine glass-doorframes so that the glazing would fit flush with the backs of the frames. Small plastic stops (available from the glass supplier) would later be screwed to the frames to hold the panels in place, allowing easy replacement should a panel break. I scraped and sanded all the frames, tacked on the quirk beads and rounded over the inside edges of the frames with a router. I also applied quirk beads around the drawer faces.

Next, I drilled holes in the back of each door for a pair of Blum 125° clip-on cup hinges. A Blum "Juniorpress" drilling fixture

A fixture attached to a drill press was used to simultaneously drill a 35mm cup hole and two 8mm attachment holes for each door hinge, as well as to press the hinges into place. Here, the author demonstrates the jig on a sample oak door.

although some distributors may still carry it. An alternative is to make pencil marks on the drilling jig itself to indicate locations of the various hardware.

Time to Finish

I cut the solid stock for the doorframes, the drawer faces, and the trim slightly oversized. After jointing the parts to final width, I used a beading bit chucked in a table-mounted router to shape the quirk-bead detail for the doors, the drawer faces, and the pelmut moldings, then switched to a chamfering bit to shape the edges of rails, pilasters, and other moldings.

attached to my drill press (photo, facing page) made it easy to drill simultaneously a 35mm cuphole and two 8mm attachment holes for each hinge. An attachment on the device allowed me to install the hinges, too. Though the Juniorpress lists for $600, I've found it to be a worthwhile investment.

Before assembling the drawers, I routed grooves in the plywood sides and fronts to hold the drawer bottoms, then used a Freud® lock-miter bit to cut the corner joints. The drawers were assembled with glue and brads, then fitted with Blum 230 bottom-mounted, self-closing drawer slides, which attach to the bottom edges of drawers for rapid installation. Drawer faces were attached with Blum drawer-face adjusters, which are plastic inserts that I install in the backs of the faces to allow adjustment for perfect alignment.

Carcase Assembly

Finally, more than 100 hours into the job, it was time to put together some cabinets. I began by fastening the hinge plates, the drawer slides, and the leg sockets to the appropriate carcase panels, then tacked the carcases together with finish nails, squared them up, and screwed on the fiberboard backs. The side panels were then secured to the tops and the bottoms with "Confirmat"® threaded-steel knockdown fasteners available from Häfele® America Co. Pilot holes were drilled using a "Zentrix 40 + 50mm"® drilling system (also available from Häfele) attached to my electric drill. This device (top photo, right) sells for about $285 and made it easy to drill perpendicular holes the proper distance from the panel edges.

Once the carcases were assembled, I flipped them onto their backs and, using a pneumatic finish nailer, installed the pilasters in the double-door openings. Then I installed the middle rails and the plywood backing for the cornice moldings. Next, I installed half-moon slide-out shelves in both corner units and a tilt-out sink tray for more

Instead of the usual tongue-and-groove assembly, these carcases are butt-joined and held together with knockdown fasteners. Here, the author demonstrates the drilling of pilot holes for the fasteners using a Häfele drilling fixture.

The two blind corners in the kitchen are fitted with half-moon slide-out shelves. The shelves swing out of the cabinets, then roll forward for easy access.

storage (bottom photo, p. 19) Designed for blind corners (corner spaces that don't turn the corner), the slide-outs swing out of the cabinet, then slide forward for easy access. The last step was to install the drawers and the doors.

Installation

To prepare for installation of the cabinets, I snapped level chalklines 34½ in. and 53½ in. up from the high point of the floor around the perimeter of the kitchen to indicate the tops of the base units and the bottoms of the upper units. I established these elevations using a reservoir-type water level from Price Brothers Tool Co., which can be operated by one person.

I installed a corner base unit first by tapping its four adjustable legs into their sockets, sliding the unit into position, and then backing out the legs until the top of the unit was level with the lower chalkline. Next, I fastened a pilaster to either end of the unit with 1¼-in. drywall screws, positioning the pilasters so that their front edges jutted ¾ in. beyond the front edge of the cabinet.

For each subsequent unit, it was a simple matter to slide the carcase against the pilasters, level it to the chalklines and screw it to the pilasters with 2-in. drywall screws. I continued around the kitchen until all the base units were in place. I then fastened them all to the wall studs with 2½-in. drywall screws angled through the top frames and into the studs, using shims to fill any gaps.

The upper units were fastened to the walls with 2½-in.-long, #10 oval-head wood screws, and to each other (through pilasters) with drywall screws. End and exposed back panels were attached to the cabinets with drywall screws driven from inside the cabinets.

I fastened the various horizontal moldings to the cases with 1¼-in. finish nails. The toekicks were then cut to length and attached to the leg levelers with plastic clips hammered into saw kerfs along the backs of the kicks. These clips allow the kicks to be removed later to trace plumbing leaks, exterminate pests, or lay a new floor.

Once the shelves were installed, the doors and the drawer faces adjusted and the porcelain pulls screwed on, I filled the visible nail holes with putty and snapped almond-colored plastic caps over the visible screw heads.

Jim Tolpin is the author of The New Cottage Home *and* The New Family Home, *both published by The Taunton Press.*

Installing Kitchen Cabinets

■ BY TOM LAW

Well, there you are, just walking into a new kitchen with freshly painted drywall. Or maybe you're remodeling, and you've spent the last few days gutting the kitchen. But now you've got a clean slate to work with. The kitchen cabinets are in cardboard boxes, and all you have to do is unpack them and fasten them to the wall, right? Easy, tiger.

Kitchen cabinets are like carry-out food: A lot can go wrong with the order, and you don't want to be five miles down the road when you discover that something's missing. Before you begin installing cabinets, check all the boxes. Make sure you have everything you need and that the cabinets are what the customer ordered.

Take a close look at the walls and the floor—they're probably not as flat as they appear. You'll have to compensate for any imperfections because the cabinets take precedence. You don't distort a straight cabinet to fit a crooked wall.

Here, I'll discuss the methods I use to install cabinets when conditions are less than perfect, and believe me, they usually are.

Starting from the high or low spot on the floor, the height of the base cabinets is marked on the wall, then the mark is transferred around the room with a water level. The line is also a reference point for laying out the upper cabinets.

Know the Room Conditions

Every installation begins with a check of the floor and the walls for the carpenter's guiding principles: plumb and level, straight and square. I use a straightedge and a level to see how the floor goes. The goal is to locate high and low spots because one of these spots will be the starting point for the cabinet layout, ultimately determining the height of the countertop.

I also use the straightedge to check the walls for straight and plumb. If there is a corner, I check it for square. Although serious flaws are uncommon, minor problems like crooked studs or spackle buildup often appear.

Marking the Wall and the Floor

To get over the fidgets of starting the job, I mark the cabinet layout on the wall. Marking the layout helps me visualize the finished job.

To begin with, I decide whether to use the high or low spot on the floor for my starting point. Choosing the high spot probably means that only one base cabinet will sit directly on the floor; all the others will be shimmed up. Using the low spot means that most of the cabinets will have to be scribed to fit the irregularities of the floor (more about scribing later). It's easier to use the high spot because it's easier to shim up than to cut off, but the determining factor is countertop height. Usually a countertop is 3 ft. from the floor.

Countertops themselves are normally 1½ in. thick, so the base cabinets are 34½ in. high. I mark this height on the wall above either the high or the low spot on the floor, whichever I've chosen as the starting point. Then I transfer that mark around the walls using a water level (photo, p. 21). I use the water level to mark the cabinet height at each corner, then I strike a chalkline between the marks. If you don't have a water level, a conventional spirit level and a straightedge will do.

After the base-cabinet line is marked on the wall, I mark the location of the individual cabinets. I usually don't mark full plumb lines (the vertical lines) for each cabinet; I just make check marks along the base-cabinet line to indicate the width of each cabinet.

The face-frame stiles on most cabinets project beyond the sides ⅛2 in. to ¼ in., which allows the stiles of two cabinets to be joined tightly without the sides of the cabinets bumping together. I mark each cabinet's actual size (its width from stile to stile) on the wall and then subtract the amount the stiles protrude to locate the back of the cabinet accurately.

I also use the base-cabinet line as a reference for laying out the upper cabinets. The space between the upper cabinets and the countertop is usually between 16 in. and 18 in. When measuring up from the base-cabinet line, I add 1½ in. for the countertop. Then I mark the wall to indicate the bottom of the upper cabinets. I double check to see that the top of the upper cabinets is the same height as the top of any full-length cabinet, like a broom closet or a pantry unit. If it isn't, I adjust the layout of the upper cabinets.

Next, I mark the location of each upper cabinet, again with either check marks or full-length lines. Most of the time the upper cabinets are the same width as the base cabinets below them, and their edges align vertically. Cabinets must line up where an appliance, such as a refrigerator, protrudes into the upper-cabinet space. And, by the way, you shouldn't add anything to the space indicated on the plans for an appliance. A 30-in. stove or refrigerator as called out on the plan will fit a 30-in. opening.

Some cabinets, such as those over refrigerators and stoves, don't come down as low as the other upper cabinets. And some cabinets, such as desk units, sit lower than the other base cabinets. I measure these cabinets and mark their locations.

Next I find the studs and mark their locations on the wall because I'll be fastening the cabinets to the studs. I mark stud locations with straight lines. Studs can be sounded out (where you tap the wall and listen for the higher pitch that occurs when you strike a stud) and probed for with a hammer and a nail, or they can be located with an electronic stud finder. If you use the hammer-and-nail approach, be sure to punch the holes where they'll be covered by cabinets.

It's OK to fasten a base cabinet to only one stud. Upper cabinets, however, are better off attached to two studs. Sometimes a cabinet isn't wide enough to catch two studs. I either attach narrow cabinets to their neighbors, or I might add blocking in the wall where it will be covered by a cabinet. I use a reciprocating saw to cut a hole in the drywall, then I insert a glue-covered piece of 1x that will span the hole. This block is the backing that I'll attach the cabinet to, so I make sure the hole is in the right place behind the cabinet.

Which Cabinets Come First?

The most important consideration when deciding which cabinets to set first, the uppers or the bases, is comfort. Some manufacturers suggest hanging the upper ones first because you can stand closer to the wall when the base cabinets aren't in the way. If you hang the upper cabinets first, it's sometimes recommended that you nail a 1x2 ledger strip on the wall to support the upper cabinets while you fasten them to the wall. It's a good idea if the backsplash will later cover the nail holes. But you wouldn't want to nail a ledger strip on a finished wall.

There are lots of ways to hold upper cabinets in place as you install them. You can buy or make various jacks and props, but it's been my experience that when hanging upper cabinets first, it's better to have two people doing the work—one holding, one fastening.

When I work alone, I find it awkward to hang upper cabinets first. By installing the base cabinets first, I can use them to support the upper cabinets (more on this method later). Plus the base cabinets are more complicated because they have to be fitted to both the wall and the floor, so I start with them.

Start from a Corner

It's much easier to start in a corner and work out of it than to put yourself in one. Most corner cabinets have their backs cut on a 45° angle, so setting them into an out-of-square corner is easy. If the cabinet has a square back, spackle buildup will probably have to be sanded down, but there are times when the only thing to do is cut away the drywall or plaster to get a square-back unit in place.

Because most corner cabinets have cutaway backs, they tend to shift around and are difficult to set in place. One way to shore up corner cabinets is to attach cabinets to each side and then push all three into place as a unit.

Another thing about corner cabinets with cutaway backs is that they often require a ledger strip along the wall to support the countertop. I nail a piece of 1x stock along the base-cabinet line to support the countertop in the corner.

Scribing a Cabinet

When a base cabinet—corner or otherwise—is installed, it must be set level and plumb. If the floor isn't level, there are two ways to get that base cabinet level and plumb—shim it or scribe it. Shimming is much easier; I

The most important consideration when deciding which cabinets to set first, the uppers or the bases, is comfort.

Shims are used to level a cabinet, but they also bring cabinets that sit in low spots of the floor up to the proper height. Here, the end cabinet of a peninsula is leveled.

just slip shims under the cabinet until it's level and at the proper height (top photo, left). When the top is level, I check all the sides; as long as the cabinet is square, the sides should be plumb no matter how I place the level. Exposed shims and gaps are often covered by a vinyl base; sometimes there's a separate toe-kick board that's scribed to fit the contours of the floor. If I'm installing base cabinets over a wood floor, I hide the shims and the gaps with shoe molding.

If the top of the cabinet is above the lay-out line even before I shim it, scribing is necessary. To scribe a cabinet to the floor, I bring the cabinet as close as I can to where it belongs in the kitchen, then shim it level. I set my scriber (or pencil compass) to the amount the cabinet extends above the line and scribe the cabinet at the floor (drawing, facing page). I cut the bottom of the cabinet at the scribe line. When I replace the cabinet, it sits level with the base-cabinet line.

Some cabinets have a separate end panel that should be scribed to fit tightly against the wall. With the panel clamped in place, the author uses a pocketknife to hold a strip of wood for scribing. The wood strip, like a scriber or compass, holds the pencil a set distance from the wall. The scribe mark is made on masking tape.

The author uses a handsaw to get a clean cut along the scribe line. A slight back cut ensures that the face of the end panel will fit tight to the wall.

Scribing a Base Cabinet

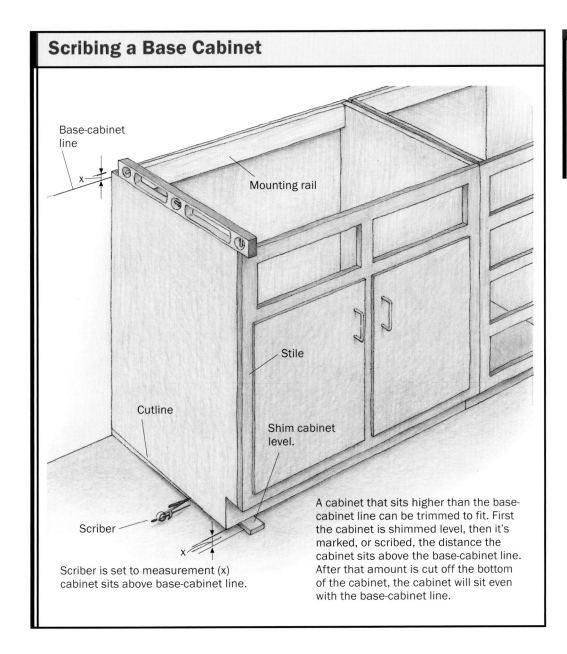

Base-cabinet line

x

Mounting rail

Stile

Cutline

Shim cabinet level.

Scriber

X

Scriber is set to measurement (x) cabinet sits above base-cabinet line.

A cabinet that sits higher than the base-cabinet line can be trimmed to fit. First the cabinet is shimmed level, then it's marked, or scribed, the distance the cabinet sits above the base-cabinet line. After that amount is cut off the bottom of the cabinet, the cabinet will sit even with the base-cabinet line.

When the side of a cabinet is exposed, it must fit perfectly against the wall. The side panels of many cabinets project beyond the back panels. These cabinets are easy to scribe to a wall. First, I level the cabinet, then set the scriber to the widest space between the cabinet and the wall and scribe both sides. I remove the cabinet, cut the sides to the scribe lines, then reinstall it. In some kitchens a decorative end panel is used to dress up the exposed side of a cabinet. Such panels are usually slightly oversized so that they can be scribed to the wall (bottom photos, facing page). If the cabinet has a flush back, however, scribing is impossible, so straightening the wall or shimming the back and covering the gap with molding is the only choice.

Installation Information

Now that I've talked about laying out and fitting cabinets to the floor and the wall, here's how I go about installing a kitchen. First, I put the corner cabinet in place, shim it level with the base-cabinet line, and, if

Cabinet stiles are clamped flush and joined with wood screws before the cabinets are installed. Two wood screws hold the cabinets together, one near each hinge.

A straightedge placed along a run of cabinets shows which cabinets must move in or out. Here, a cabinet is pried away from the wall and shimmed out.

necessary, scribe the cabinet to fit. Then I fasten the cabinet to the wall by driving screws through the mounting rail into the wall studs. The mounting rail is a horizontal piece of wood at the back of the cabinet.

Screws need to bite into studs at least ¾ in., so I use 2½-in. or 3-in. long drywall screws. But you may prefer to use wood screws, which have thicker shanks, or use the screws supplied by the manufacturer. If there's a gap between the mounting rail and the wall right where I want to run a screw, I slip a shim into the gap to keep the back of the cabinet from distorting when I put in the screw.

After the first cabinet is in place, I bring the second one to it, level it, get the face frames flush by lining up the top and the bottom of the cabinet's stiles, then I clamp the stiles together.

When the stiles are flush and tight with each other, I fasten them with screws (top left photo). I always drill pilot holes and countersink the screws. Usually two screws in each stile are sufficient. When the doors are closed, the screws are hidden, but I still try to make them inconspicuous when the doors are open by putting the screws close to the hinges. Once the adjoining stiles are screwed together, I screw the cabinet to the wall.

I install each succeeding base cabinet the same way—level it, shim or scribe as required, fasten the stiles, and then screw it to the wall. As the run of cabinets grows, I put a straightedge across the front of the cabinets to make sure they're in line (photo, top right). I make any adjustments at the wall by tightening or loosening screws and adding shims.

Installing a Sink Base

Sink base cabinets with back panels may be more difficult to install because they might have to be bored for plumbing and electrical lines. If the cabinets on each side of the sink base are in position—even temporarily—I use them as reference points from which to measure the locations of pipes and wires.

If the surrounding cabinets aren't in place, I mark the sink base-cabinet layout full size on both the wall and the floor. Then I can measure the pipe and wire locations from the layout lines.

If I drill holes in the back of the cabinet from behind, I complete them from the finished side to avoid tearing out the veneer. A little tearout isn't a big deal because the plumber usually puts a finish plate around the opening that covers a rough cut.

Some sink base cabinets have no back panel; obviously it won't be necessary to drill holes if the pipes and the wires come through the wall. But sometimes they come up through the floor. And that's when the layout lines on the floor come in handy.

Installing between Walls

When a run of base cabinets fits between walls, the dimensions may work out, and the cabinets will fit exactly. But more often than not, the cabinets will require some fitting.

If the total dimension of the cabinets is just slightly more than the space to be filled, I put all the cabinets in except the last one, and I leave the next-to-last cabinet unattached; that is, I don't screw it to the wall yet. I measure the space left for the last cabinet. Then I remove the next-to-last one and put the last one back in plumb and level. I scribe it to fit the return wall. The amount of material to be scribed off the last cabinet's stile will be determined by the space required for the next-to-last cabinet when it's replaced.

This strip of wood acts as a spacer to hold the corner cabinets far enough apart so that their drawers don't bump into each other.

TIP

To help the cabinet slide in without marring the finish, use wax paper between the stiles.

Once all the scribing and trimming is complete, I put the last cabinet in place, then push the next-to-last cabinet in place with a pry bar. I use wax paper between the stiles to help the cabinet slide in without marring the finish.

Installing Filler and Backer Strips

When a run of cabinets doesn't quite fill the space between walls, filler strips are used. A filler strip is simply a board of the same kind of wood and finish as the cabinets, and it gets screwed to a cabinet's stile to fill a gap. Sometimes cabinets can be ordered with wider stiles to make up the difference, but fillers are more common.

To scribe a filler strip, I first screw it onto the cabinet stile, move the cabinet as close as possible to its final position, then I scribe, using the widest gap as the amount to cut

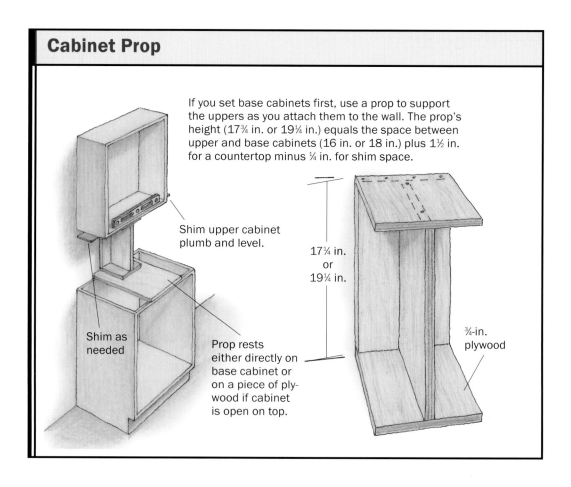

Cabinet Prop

If you set base cabinets first, use a prop to support the uppers as you attach them to the wall. The prop's height (17¾ in. or 19¼ in.) equals the space between upper and base cabinets (16 in. or 18 in.) plus 1½ in. for a countertop minus ¼ in. for shim space.

Shim upper cabinet plumb and level.

Shim as needed

Prop rests either directly on base cabinet or on a piece of plywood if cabinet is open on top.

17¼ in. or 19¼ in.

¾-in. plywood

Cabinet jacks consist of square steel tubes that slide inside each other; a cabinet sits in a cushioned angle iron.

off. I almost always leave a filler strip on a cabinet and cut the strip in place.

Backer strips are frequently installed at inside corners to keep cabinets as far enough apart so that drawers or drawer handles don't bump into each other. Because the cabinets have to be separated by the thickness of the drawer front and the hardware, fastening a backer strip to the abutting cabinet will increase the clearance (photo, p. 27). We'll run into an inside corner later when I talk about peninsulas. But right now, I've still got to hang the upper cabinets.

Installing Upper Cabinets

Like the base cabinets, upper cabinets should be installed level and plumb, with sides parallel and stiles screwed together. All of the cabinets should be fastened to the wall using the same screws as those used for the base cabinets. I like to drive two screws in the top mounting rail and two into the bottom mounting rail. I fill gaps between the wall and the cabinet with shims as needed.

When hanging big, heavy upper cabinets, I lighten the load by removing all doors and shelves, and I reinstall whatever I've removed when all the cabinets are set. Removing the doors before hanging the cabinets also makes it easier to clamp the stiles together before driving the screws.

Instead of holding the cabinets in place as I try to fasten them to the wall, I typically use some plywood props (drawing, facing page) or adjustable cabinet jacks (photo, facing page). I made two different-size props from ¾-in plywood; one prop is 17¼ in. high for a 16-in. spacing between upper and base cabinets; the other is 19¼ in. high for an 18-in. spacing (16 in. and 18 in. are the two most popular spacings between upper cabinets and base cabinets). The finish space between upper and base cabinets is 16 in. or 18 in.; the additional 1¼ in. on each prop makes up for the countertop that's not yet in place. The missing ¼ in. is shim space. I put a prop on a base cabinet and rest an upper cabinet on the prop. I use long shims to adjust the height of the upper cabinet to the layout line. (Some base cabinets are open on top, so I lay a piece of plywood on top of these cabinets and use the shorter props.)

Just as I installed the base cabinets, I start with a corner cabinet and work my way out. Each succeeding cabinet is put into place on the plywood prop and shimmed level. Then I clamp and screw the stiles together. Finally I screw the cabinet to the wall and remove the prop.

The fronts of the upper cabinets should also be checked with a straightedge and adjusted at the wall line, again either by tightening screws or backing them out and adding shims.

Islands and Peninsulas

When the kitchen plan includes an island or a peninsula, I make a full-size layout on the floor and check the squareness of the corner with the old 3-4-5 triangle. If the finish floor isn't down yet, I snap chalklines. But if the finish floor is in place, I don't want chalk everywhere, so I use masking tape to show where the cabinets go.

An island or a peninsula should be secured to the floor, and I do it by screwing 1x blocks to the floor, then placing the cabinets over the blocks and screwing the cabinets to the blocks (drawing, below).

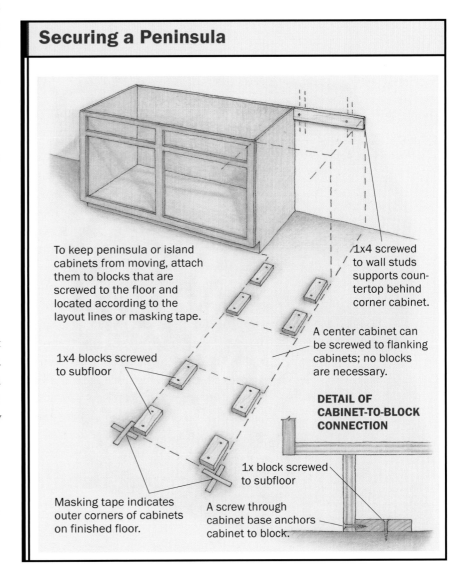

Securing a Peninsula

To keep peninsula or island cabinets from moving, attach them to blocks that are screwed to the floor and located according to the layout lines or masking tape.

1x4 blocks screwed to subfloor

Masking tape indicates outer corners of cabinets on finished floor.

1x4 screwed to wall studs supports countertop behind corner cabinet.

A center cabinet can be screwed to flanking cabinets; no blocks are necessary.

DETAIL OF CABINET-TO-BLOCK CONNECTION

1x block screwed to subfloor

A screw through cabinet base anchors cabinet to block.

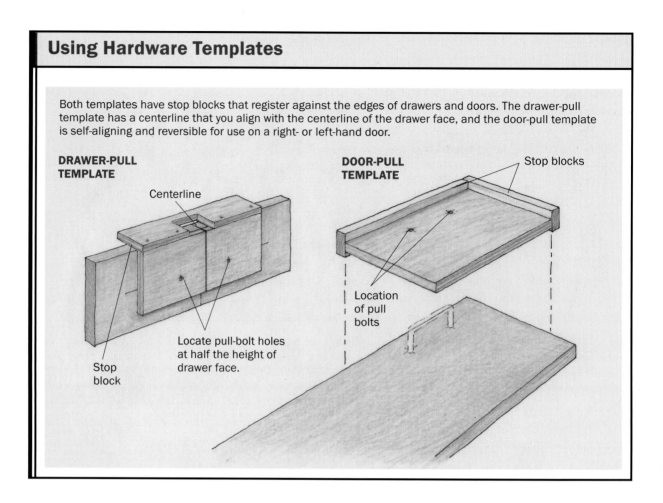

Both templates have stop blocks that register against the edges of drawers and doors. The drawer-pull template has a centerline that you align with the centerline of the drawer face, and the door-pull template is self-aligning and reversible for use on a right- or left-hand door.

DRAWER-PULL TEMPLATE

Centerline

Locate pull-bolt holes at half the height of drawer face.

Stop block

DOOR-PULL TEMPLATE

Stop blocks

Location of pull bolts

Using my layout lines, I measure in from the edge of the masking tape or chalkline (which represents the outside of the cabinet) and mark the thickness of the cabinet's base. The new marks indicate where to screw the blocks down. Usually I just use a 6-in. to 8-in. block of 1x4 in each corner. Before I screw the cabinet to the blocks, I shim or scribe the cabinet so that it's plumb, level and at the same height as the other cabinets. When an island or a peninsula cabinet is placed over the blocks, it can't be shifted side to side, and when the screws go through the cabinet into the blocks, it can't be lifted either.

Hardware and Handles

After I've replaced all the doors and the drawers, I install the hardware. If the holes for the pulls have been predrilled, it's easy enough to screw the hardware on. But if I need to drill the holes myself, and there are a lot of holes to drill, it's best to make a template (drawing, above). I use a piece of plywood and glue a stop block at its edge, which holds the template in place on the door or the drawer.

I sometimes use masking tape to mark the hole centers. Masking tape makes pencil marks more visible, but I double check the marks by holding the handle up to them. I use a sharp scratch awl or punch to mark the hole, then drill it through. The center punch keeps the drill bit from wandering.

Tom Law lives in Westminster, Maryland. His video on installing kitchen cabinets is available from The Taunton Press.

Installing European Cabinets

Cabinetry manufactured in Europe brought both a new look and a new installation system to the United States. European cabinets are frameless—they have no face frame—and the shelf pins, the hardware mounting screws, and the dowels that join the carcases are drilled on 32mm centers. Although many American cabinet manufacturers have incorporated the European look and construction system into their lines, few have fully incorporated its installation system.

Laying out the cabinet

European cabinetry has its own suspension and support hardware that makes installing cabinets fast and efficient, even if you work alone. Upper cabinets are hung from a steel rail that you screw to the wall studs. Base cabinets stand on adjustable leveling legs. Thanks to this hardware, plumbing and leveling cabinets are much simpler.

When laying out a European kitchen, I snap three level lines on the walls. One line indicates the top of the base cabinet; one line indicates the bottom of the upper cabinets, and the third line is for the upper cabinets' hanging rail. The height of this rail varies from brand to brand.

The hanging rail is a length of steel about 1¼ in. wide with an offset bend along the top edge. I predrill ¼-in. holes at 5cm o.c. (about 2 in. o.c.; European cabinetry is all metric). I screw the rail to the wall through these holes with #14 2½-in. pan-head screws.

Upper cabinets first

I install the upper cabinets first. They hang on the channel in the hanging rail via a pair of adjustable hooks (photos, right) that protrude from the back of each cabinet. Two

A hanging rail screwed to the studs supports upper cabinets that have adjustable leveling hooks. This system allows one person to install cabinets.

(continued)

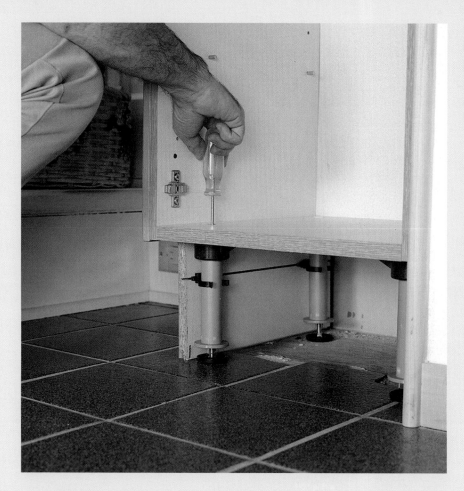

You don't have to shim or scribe European cabinets because they rest on legs that are adjusted up or down with a screwdriver. The toekick clips onto the legs; the clips are also adjustable.

set screws on each hook adjust the wall cabinets. One screw moves the cabinet in and out; the other moves the cabinet up and down. With this system, one person can easily hang and adjust wall cabinets.

When the hanging rail is above the cabinets, crown molding conceals it. If the hanging rail runs behind the cabinets, I notch the back of the cabinets to fit over the rail. However, end cabinets with visible side panels aren't notched; the hanging rail stops against the inside edge of a visible side panel.

Once the upper cabinets are aligned, I bolt them together using joining bolts supplied by the manufacturer. Most

European cabinets have partially bored holes inside along the front of the side panels. I clamp the cabinets together, finish drilling the holes and then pass the bolts through. The bolts are similar to small carriage bolts with a threaded cap or socket. All of the European cabinets I've seen come with these bolts. If the cabinets you're installing come without bolts, you can use short drywall screws.

Then the base cabinets

Base cabinets have leveling legs that slip into plastic sockets on the bottom of the cabinet. The legs usually come with each cabinet, along with caps that cover adjustment access holes in the cabinet floor. To level and plumb a cabinet, I either use the access holes to turn the legs with a screwdriver (photo, facing page), or I turn the legs by hand.

Europeans don't fasten base cabinets to the wall. The thinking is that because base cabinets are joined together and attached to countertops and appliances, the cabinets won't move. Also, Europeans take their cabinets with them when they move, so fewer screws going in during installation means fewer screws to take out on moving day.

I like to be sure that my cabinets will stay put, so I fasten them to the wall. How I fasten them depends on the brand of cabinet I'm installing. True European cabinets are a bit shallower than the typical 2-ft.-deep face-frame cabinet. When I install European cabinets, I space them away from the wall slightly so that they'll be the right depth for a conventional countertop. Some manufacturers supply special particleboard blocks with their cabinets that are screwed to the wall and to the cabinet, serving as both a spacer block and a rigid means of attachment.

If the manufacturer doesn't supply blocking, I screw a 2x4 cleat to the wall at the level line and fasten the cabinets to the cleat. I use a length of predrilled metal angle inside each cabinet to keep the wall-mounting screws from pulling through the back panel.

Finally, install the toekick

Toekick material, usually particleboard covered with plastic laminate or veneer to match the cabinets, comes in long lengths about 7 in. wide. I rip it to the proper width.

If the finish flooring is not in place, I rip the toekick narrow enough to accommodate the flooring. Or better yet, I cut and install the toekick after the flooring has been installed. A vinyl sealer strip (similar to weatherstripping) comes either attached or loose to seal the bottom edge of the toekick to the floor.

After cutting the toekick to length, I join inside and outside corners with plastic end caps. If corners join at angles other than 90°, I miter the toekicks and glue the joints. The toekick is grooved on the back to accept knock-in clips that grip the leveling legs. To install the clips, I lay the toekick face down on the floor in front of and aligned with the cabinets, and then I mark the location of every other leg and pop in the clips. The clips consist of a T-shaped knock-in and a U-shaped clip that slides over the knock-in. This combination allows some side-to-side adjustment of the toekick once it's pressed onto the legs. End caps then snap onto the kick ends.

Island and peninsula cabinets are freestanding and are likely to tip and sway. To anchor these cabinets to the floor, I make L-shaped plywood brackets. The vertical side of the L is about two-thirds the height of the toekick. I use these brackets in pairs, usually two pairs per cabinet. I screw one bracket to the floor and the other to the bottom of the cabinet, installing them so that the vertical faces of the brackets ride against each other. Then I set the cabinets in place, level them, join them, and screw the brackets together.

Tom Santarsiero is a cabinetmaker and president of The Kitchen Design Center in Montclair, New Jersey

Building Kitchen Cabinets on Site

■ BY JOSEPH B. LANZA

Back when I had a small cabinet shop in Connecticut, I built kitchens the old-fashioned way, the right way. Although beautiful when finished, the cabinets took forever to build. Over time, I slowly modernized my methods. But I was really making only minor refinements of an essentially antique process. Then I had the good luck of moving to Austin, Texas.

I worked briefly for a man named Paris Carroll, a craftsman with no fear of technology. He came to each kitchen-cabinet job with a stack of plywood, preripped face-frame stock, a few basic tools, and plenty of pneumatic nailers. Everything was glued and nailed. If I was a bit skeptical at first, it didn't take long to see that his cabinets were solid and fit beautifully. What amazed me most was how fast they went together.

After I finished school in Austin and moved back to stodgy New England, I built a few kitchens with overlay doors and cup hinges using many of Paris's techniques. I couldn't imagine going back to my old methods. When a project came along that called for the traditional look of face-frame cabinets with flush-fit doors, I started looking for a faster way to build them. Borrowing heavily from what I had learned in Austin, I

figured out how to make site-built cabinets that look every bit as traditional as cabinets painstakingly built in a custom shop.

Make the Face Frames after the Doors Have Been Hung

My cabinets consist of plywood boxes tied together with two layers of face frame: a structural subframe made from poplar and a finished face frame in the same wood species as doors, drawer fronts, and trim. Face frames are assembled with butt joints, glue, and air-driven nails, but because joints overlap each other, the finished cabinets are amazingly strong and rigid.

The proper door hinge is important. Face-frame cup hinges result in a door overlay of at least ½ in., and the doors never sit quite flush. I knew they wouldn't work. Half-overlay cup hinges made for frameless cabinets, on the other hand, are adjustable from front to back as well as up and down and from side to side. They mount on the cabinet side, not on the face frame, and result in a door overlay of about ⅜ in.

It may seem backward at first, but I hang the doors after the subframe has been in-

Using plywood or melamine boxes, these cabinets are built on site and look every bit as finely crafted as shop-built cabinets.

stalled. Then the finish face frame is added, piece by piece, around the doors. It's much faster than the traditional method of hanging inset doors in a finished cabinet. When you do it the old-fashioned way, you have to hang a door on butt hinges, check the fit, take the door out to plane it and then hang it again. And again. It's a tedious process at best. Now I can make adjustments on small pieces that are easy to run through a table saw or small jointer before they are attached. Cabinets are finished in place when they're all done, either with a spray gun or by hand.

A fair question is how these site-built cabinets compare with what you can buy. I've found that even with a staggering array of manufactured kitchen cabinets to choose

from, it can be difficult to find the right product. Sizes of manufactured kitchens are usually limited, and the fit and finish may not be what the customer wants. Several manufacturers and many local shops will build cabinets to any dimension, but this flexibility has high costs. Shop-built cabinets also may require extended lead times and precise planning. Dimensions that vary even a little from drawings cause big headaches. (Ever try to plane $\frac{3}{16}$ in. off a $\frac{3}{4}$-in. plywood cabinet side?)

By building cabinets on site, I get finished cabinets with a finely crafted, "meant-to-be-there" look, and the process is speedy.

Joseph B. Lanza is a designer and builder in Duxbury, Massachusetts.

Use Melamine or Plywood to Build Cabinet Boxes

Base cabinets for site-built kitchen cabinets start with simple carcases made from ¾-in. particleboard-core melamine or a shop-grade hardwood plywood. Although plywood is lighter and somewhat stronger, melamine is less expensive, and it needs no additional finish. For cabinets with adjustable shelves, the author often uses melamine predrilled for shelf pins. These base units, without face frames, are 22½ in. deep and 29¾ in. tall. With a toe-kick and a 1½-in. allowance for the countertop, the cabinets will be a standard 36 in. tall and 24 in. deep. Wall units are also built from ¾-in. material.

Even if pieces have been cut correctly, a cabinet box can rack slightly as it is assembled or moved. A piece of ¼-in. plywood glued and nailed to the backside of the box stiffens the assembly and squares it up.

Each cabinet component is a three-sided box. Cabinet floors are cut the full width of the box, and the sides are then glued and nailed from below. Stretchers and a hanging rail are made of 1x3 poplar.

With the back glued and nailed in place, the author uses a router and a flush-trimming bit to cut off excess plywood. Stacking boxes on top of each other saves wear and tear on back and knees.

Set Boxes on a Level Base

These cabinet boxes have no integral toe-kick. Instead, they are set on a narrower base that creates one. The author makes bases from ¾-in. plywood glued and nailed together. He dimensions them so that they provide a 4-in. high by 3-in. deep toekick once the finish floor has been installed. After checking the floor for level, he makes the bases to the smallest dimension—it's much easier to shim up the base than it is to scribe and cut it down. Bases are attached to the floor with 2x4 blocking screwed to the subfloor. Spraying the faces of the base with flat black enamel before cabinet boxes are installed makes the base virtually invisible later.

By shimming between cabinets with strips of plywood, the author creates a solid foundation for a 2¼-in.-wide poplar subframe. Back spacers, glued and nailed as cabinet boxes are set, should extend all the way to the floor for additional support.

Even a large kitchen island, such as this 12-ft.-long unit, can be handled by a single person because it is made of a number of smaller components.

Screws unify the boxes. Countersunk screw heads are hard to see when the cabinets are completed. Three 2-in. screws along the inside of each box, front and back, are plenty.

A Subframe Holds the Whole Thing Together

A finished run of cabinets is amazingly strong, in part because cabinet boxes are tied together with a subframe made of ¾-in. poplar glued and nailed in place. The three horizontal pieces (top, bottom, and drawer rails) span the full length of the run. Vertical pieces fill the spaces between them. Most of the poplar subframe will be covered later with a finish face frame. But a reveal about ⅜ in. wide will form door and drawer stops, so the author keeps nails inside this imaginary line as he attaches the pieces with a 16-ga. finish nailer.

Strong Plywood Drawers with Simple Joinery

Working with ½-in. Baltic-birch plywood, the author builds drawers on site. Using void-free plywood with thin hardwood plies makes it possible to leave edges unbanded. The author uses a roundover bit on a router table to relieve both inside and outside edges on the top of the drawer sides. Drawer bottoms are ¼-in. hardwood plywood. Corner joints can be cut on a table saw with only a few setups and little fiddling. Completed drawer boxes are glued and brad-nailed at the corners. To make assembly easier, the author rips the drawer back so that the drawer bottom can slide beneath it.

Tenons on the mating drawer pieces are exactly the thickness of the saw kerf and as long as the slot in the drawer sides. Tenons are cut in several passes on a table saw. Aim for a snug fit.

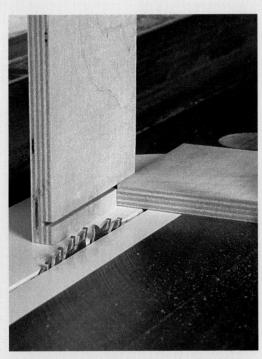

The first step is to cut a saw kerf at the front and back of each drawer side. The slot offset should equal the thickness of the plywood that will be used for drawer fronts and backs.

With yellow glue and a couple of brads, this simple joint should last a long time. With joinery completed, the author cuts the groove for the plywood bottom in a couple of passes on a table saw.

Installing Drawer Slides and Hanging the Doors

Ordinarily, a cabinet gets its face frame before doors are cut and trimmed to fit. Not here. With only a poplar subframe in place, the author next turns to doors and drawers. Finish drawer fronts, which are made on site, are added later, after the face frame has been installed. A number of companies make cabinet doors. These doors came from the Cabinet Factory in La Crosse, Wisconsin, and cost about $11 per sq. ft. of door. The author uses top-quality full-extension drawer slides.

Cup hinges attach to plates that are screwed to the insides of the cabinets. A jig for predrilling holes in the cabinet speeds the installation process considerably. This jig works for both top and bottom hinge plates.

If the jig has been made correctly, hinge parts will align, and doors should snap right into place. These Blum hinges allow the door to be adjusted in three directions for a perfect fit.

A length of 12-in.-wide flooring that has been cut to the right length and then stood inside the cabinet makes an effective support for a long drawer slide as it is screwed to the cabinet side.

An easy way to get doors aligned perfectly is to joint a long piece of wood and rest it on door tops. The author can then work his way down the cabinet, using the hinge adjustments to even the doors.

The Face Frame Completes the Cabinet

With doors hung and aligned, the author adds the finish face frame. Keeping reveals between face-frame pieces and doors consistent, ordinarily a fussy process with inset doors, is easy because the face frame is added one piece at a time. If gaps between doors are not perfectly consistent, face-frame pieces can be tapered slightly with a hand plane or on a jointer. The author starts with full-length stiles at both ends of the cabinet, adds a one-piece top rail, and then fills in with the drawer rails and the shorter stiles between doors. He uses a brad nailer and yellow glue to attach pieces.

Running a screw through the hole that will be used for the pull holds the drawer front in place temporarily. When the drawer looks right, the author opens it and then runs in two screws from the inside.

Overlay doors look like traditional inset doors when the author adds the finish face frame. When filling in short pieces, cutting one end at a slight bevel helps to ensure a tight fit.

Faux Fridge Front

■ BY MIKE GUERTIN

From the start, our kitchen plans included a refrigerator that looked like part of the cabinetry. After looking at the price tags on several models designed to accommodate cabinet-matching door panels and built-in dimensions, I had to find a better way.

Solving the depth problem was easy because I was building the cabinets myself; I just framed the refrigerator cabinet deeper to accommodate a standard refrigerator. I avoided, however, thinking about the panel-mounting problem until the last minute. My wife vetoed the idea of screwing or gluing the panels to the refrigerator doors. Defacing a brand-new appliance just wasn't an option. Then, in a moment of frustration and desperation, came a little inspiration.

Wood Doors Hang on Aluminum Channels

My plan involved metal channels shaped like a J. The channels are screwed to the backs of the wood panels and wrap around the refrigerator door (drawing, left).

I started with some leftover flat aluminum 0.032-in. gutter stock finished black. I figured the dark color would tend to draw less visual attention to the edges of the refrigerator door than a lighter color. I own a brake for bending aluminum, but for those who don't, finding someone to fabricate the channel shouldn't be a problem.

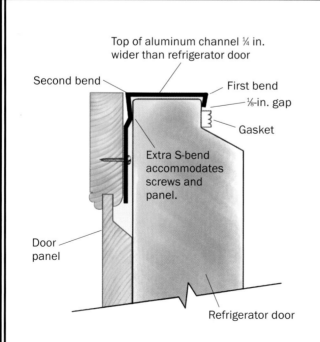

Cross Section of Panel Attachment

Top of aluminum channel ¼ in. wider than refrigerator door

Second bend

First bend

⅛-in. gap

Gasket

Extra S-bend accommodates screws and panel.

Door panel

Refrigerator door

First, I measured the distance from the gasket to the edge of the door and subtracted ⅛ in. so that the aluminum wouldn't interfere with the gasket. That was my first bend (drawing, facing page).

I made my second bend at 2½ in. (¼ in. more than the thickness of the door) to wrap around the door. The extra width makes it easier to slide the channels over the doors. On the leg that attached to the panel, I added a gentle S-bend. That bend accommodates the screws and the raised panel.

After testing one channel on the edge of the refrigerator door, I decided to overbend each 90° angle by 1° or 2° for a snug fit. I cut and bent three pieces for each door, one for each side and the top. The top channels are 2 in. short to avoid the refrigerator-door hinges (left photo, p. 44). Because the side channels extend to the bottom of each panel, I didn't put a channel on the underside of the doors.

When I had the wood panels made, I oversized them ¼ in. in both directions.

Aluminum channel is the key. Bent into a J-shape, aluminum channel is screwed to the back of the cabinet panel. A gap in the top channel accommodates the refrigerator-door hinge.

Held in place by gravity and friction. With the door removed, the panel slides easily over the door.

When I screwed the channels to each door panel, the side channels ended up a little farther apart than the actual width of the doors. That extra space kept me from having to force the panels over the doors.

Remove the Door for Easy Installation

Before I could install the panels, I had to remove the doors from the refrigerator. Otherwise the hinge brackets were in the way. With the doors removed, the wood panels slid easily over the refrigerator doors (right photo, above).

I rehung the doors on their hinges, adjusted them in the opening and pushed the refrigerator back into its cabinet. It only

took about 20 minutes to remove the refrigerator and freezer doors, slip the panels on and rehang them—not even long enough to worry about melting my Ben & Jerry's®.

The only drawback to the system was that the hinges weren't meant to accommodate the extra thickness of the clad door, so we keep the fridge sticking out slightly from the cabinet face frame to let the doors open fully. Friction and gravity keep the door panels in place. If my wife ever decides to redecorate the kitchen, I can easily slip the wood panels off and give the refrigerator a fresh white look.

Fine Homebuilding *contributing editor Mike Guertin is a builder and a building consultant in East Greenwich, Rhode Island. He is a co-author of* Precision Framing *and author of* Roofing with Asphalt Shingles, *published by The Taunton Press.*

Installing Kitchen Cabinets

■ BY KEVIN LUDDY

In Jonathan Swift's novel *Gulliver's Travels,* the Lilliputians were at war with their neighbors over whether a boiled egg should be cracked from the pointy end or from the round end. At teatime, the British squabble over whether the tea or the milk goes into the cup first. Likewise, on job sites I've seen carpenters argue vehemently about which kitchen cabinets should be installed first, lowers or uppers. There are good reasons for each choice, but you'll have to read on to find out which way I prefer.

Check Everything before Installation Begins

With this kitchen (and with all of my kitchen jobs), I received an information packet from the designer. This packet included the floor plan and elevations that showed backsplash and crown-molding heights, as well as countertop dimensions and the specs of the four built-in appliances.

All this information helps me to bid the job accurately, but I also use it during instal-lation. My first task at the site was to check the stock numbers of the cabinets against

the floor plan to make sure the order was complete and correct. I also looked at the cabinets for any obvious damage and arranged them in order of installation and by area (e.g., the island cabinets all together).

The Starting Line

The floor is first checked for level (1). The cabinet height is measured from the high point, and a level line is drawn. The same height is measured from the low point (2), and a second line is drawn (3) to find the difference and to check the first line. The first base cabinet is set and shimmed to the top line (4).

Next I measured everything in the kitchen, checking my measurements against the floor plans and elevations. I checked wall heights and lengths, locations of lights and outlets, and window and door locations; I also checked the walls for plumb and straight. The only major problem I found in my investigation was an out-of-place outlet, and lucky for me, an electrician was on site that day.

Two Lines Set the Cabinet Height

After checking the floor for level (photo 1, above), I measured up the height of the base cabinets (in this case 34½ in.) from the high spot for each run of cabinets and drew a level line across the wall with a 4-ft. level. A laser level would also work well

Joining Cabinets

Face frames are clamped flush (5) and then screwed together. A framing square clamped to the cabinet (6) keeps tall cabinets square to shorter ones. Tall cabinets are plumbed (7) and then screwed to the wall. Cabinets are kept level while they're being joined (8).

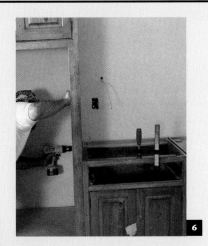

here. I don't recommend snapping chalk-lines, though. They're usually too fuzzy and not always level.

Next, I found the low spot for each run, measured up the same distance (photo 2, facing page) and drew a second line (photo 3), which gave me the range of floor error and checked the accuracy of my first line. If the lines are parallel, I'm all set. If not, I go back and try it again. The finished kitchen floor (½-in. tile over ⅜-in. subfloor) had not been installed, so I could count on it to hide shims. (Otherwise, I would have had to undercut, or scribe, every base cabinet, which is time-consuming.) The top line then became my guide for cabinet level.

I then marked the stud locations along the level line. I also located critical points such as the window centerline. Some carpenters mark the location of each cabinet along the level line, but I usually scrunch the exact locations by fractions as I go to make everything fit, which would render those marks wrong.

The Base Cabinets Go in First

Installing base cabinets first takes a little more care, but I use the lowers to help with installing the uppers. Besides, most bad surprises show up when installing the lowers.

For this kitchen, I began with the lazy-Susan corner cabinet. I transferred the stud locations to the back of the cabinet and drilled screw holes through the hanging strip for every stud location.

Then I placed the cabinet in the corner, shimmed it plumb and level (photo 4, p. 46), and drove a #10 by 2½-in. pan-head screw through each hole. I steer clear of using drywall screws when I'm attaching cabinets because they have little shear resistance. Then I laid out and drilled the screw holes for the cabinet to the left of the corner and slid it into place.

To join the two cabinets, I first clamped the face frames together, lining up the faces and the tops flush. Next I shimmed the cabinet plumb and level, and joined the face frames with screws through predrilled holes. I finished by screwing the cabinet to the wall.

This kitchen had a full-height wall-oven cabinet next in line. To attach the cabinet, I joined the face frames as before (photo 5, p. 47) but clamped a framing square to the top of the base cabinet to keep the oven cabinet square to its neighbor (photo 6). I then plumbed the other side of the oven cabinet (photo 7) and drove screws top and bottom to hold it in place.

Fridge Cabinet Is Assembled on Site

On the other side of the corner, I leveled and installed a double-drawer base cabinet (photo 8). The fridge cabinet that came next had to be built on site from factory-supplied parts.

I began by setting the overhead cabinet on its side. Next I positioned one side panel on the overhead cabinet, supporting its loose end on a base cabinet. After lining up the top and front edges, I screwed through the panel and into the cabinet.

After carefully flipping over the unit, I installed the opposite side panel (photo 9, facing page), this time using trim screws. With the unit assembled, I lifted it and rotated it into place (photo 10). Like most refrigerator cabinets, this one was deeper than the base cabinets. I plumbed and leveled the cabinet and then screwed the left side into the face frame of the adjoining base cabinet.

Holding the unit plumb, I screwed the overhead cabinet into the studs. To stabilize the sides and to keep them at the proper width, I screwed two spreader cleats to the wall, one at the floor and another at the height of the base cabinets (photo 11). A trim screw anchored the side panel to the cleats. The finish floor will lock the bottoms of the panels firmly in place.

Bevel Cut Makes a Tight Scribe

This kitchen had two other cabinet runs, a freestanding island, and cabinets along an outside wall for the kitchen sink, dishwasher, and trash compactor. The kitchen-sink base had to fit over a toe-kick heater and accept an unusual sink, so I assembled it from parts supplied by the cabinet company (sidebar, p. 50).

The sink base had a fixed width, so I marked out its dimensions centered on the window. Next I double-checked all the clearance specs and left the correct space on both sides of the sink base for the appliances. On the right side of the dishwasher, I installed a wine-rack end panel screwed to a 2x cleat on the wall.

The cabinet on the other side of the trash compactor had a preattached filler piece that had to be scribed to make the cabinet fit properly. To mark the scribe, I first set the cabinet in place and shimmed it level and plumb. Then I set my compass scribes and marked the cut on the filler piece (photo 12, p. 51).

Building the Fridge Cabinet

The refrigerator cabinet is made from two side panels joined to a top cabinet (9). The cabinet is carefully positioned (10) and attached to its neighbor. Wall cleats hold the sides at the proper width (11).

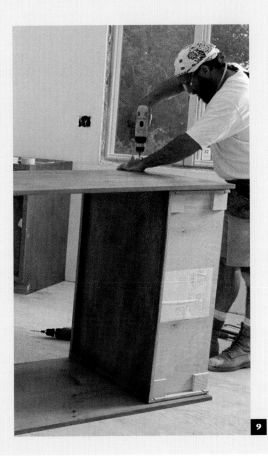

I try to put a slight bevel on all my scribe cuts, so I tipped the saw table slightly as I followed the line (photo 13). Masking tape on the bottom of the saw helps to protect the cabinet. The bevel cut lets the cabinet fit more tightly against the wall (photo 14). If the cut needs fine-tuning, I do it with an electric grinder. When I was happy with the fit, I screwed the cabinet into place. Note that with a wider filler piece, a wall cleat may be needed for attachment.

Blocks Anchor the Island in Place

Islands and peninsulas are special situations because the cabinets don't attach to walls. For this island, I began by snapping chalklines on the floor, laying out the full perimeter of the island.

One side of this island had a standard toekick, but the other side was to be covered with a solid beadboard panel. On the toe-

A Sink Cabinet from Factory-Supplied Parts

While writing a song, a friend once asked me how many Ps there were in "obstacle," as though it rhymed with pop-sicle. Of course, there are no Ps in "obstacle," but there were many obstacles to using a stock cabinet at the sink location in this kitchen project.

In addition to the plumbing pipes, it was to receive a specialty sink, and it sat over a toekick heater vent. With all these variables, the designers opted to build the cabinet on site from factory-supplied parts.

I started by building the toekick of 2x stock ripped to a height that would fit the vent cover supplied to me. It was slightly taller than the standard toekick, but the difference would be seen only by the bristles on the kitchen broom. With the appropriate gap left for the vent, I squared and leveled the base, centered it under the window, and glued and screwed it to the floor (bottom left photo).

The base platform went on next, followed by the sides (top right photo). I cut the lower front corners of the side pieces to match the toekick on the rest of the kitchen. A 1x wall cleat anchored the sides in back.

Building the sink base from parts meant not having to drill holes for the plumbing, but when drilling is necessary, I measure the vertical location from my level line on the wall. I take the horizontal location from the adjacent cabinet and transfer this information to the back of the sink base, remembering to subtract for any face-frame overhangs. Next, I bore halfway through from the backside and then finish the hole from the inside.

The final step was installing the finished front, which was glued and tacked to the sides (bottom right photo). It looked a little funny when I was done, but I knew that with the countertop, sink, and appliances in place, you'd never be able to tell that the cabinet was built on site.

Scribing an Attached Filler

Cabinets with attached fillers have to be scribed to fit. With the cabinet in place, the cut is traced onto the filler (12). Next, the cut is made with the saw tipped to create a bevel (13), which lets the cabinet fit tight against the wall (14).

kick side, I subtracted the toekick depth and the thickness of the cabinet wall and snapped a second line. I also marked where the cabinets were joined together. I then glued and screwed 2x blocks to the floor at the ends of the island and along the toekick, leaving plenty of space where the cabinets would be joined (photo 15, p. 52).

Next I ran a bead of construction adhesive on the blocks where they would contact the cabinets and then slipped the cabinets over the blocks. The cabinets were then clamped and screwed together in the front and back (photo 16), keeping the whole assembly level and square. I screwed the cabinets to the blocks along the toe-kick (photo 17) where the screws would be hidden and drove the trim screws through the end panels to hold them in place until the glue cured. The beadboard panel went on next (photo 18), and the island was solid as a rock.

Upper Cabinets Ride Piggyback on the Bases

With all the lower cabinets in place, the final step before moving to the upper cabinets was installing countertop support cleats as needed. The first upper cabinet I set in was the corner unit that was to rest on the countertop. I blocked the corner unit to the thickness of the countertop and made sure that it was absolutely plumb and level. I also checked the distance to the other cabinets. The corner cabinet was left loose with the idea that I could slide it up and out of the way when the countertop was installed and then drop it down for a precise fit on the granite counter.

For this kitchen, the refrigerator cabinet and the oven cabinet set the height of the

Assembling the Island

After chalklines are snapped for the island, 2x blocks are glued and screwed inside the perimeter (15). The cabinets are then glued to the blocks and joined front and back (16). Screws driven into the blocks from the front (17) will be hidden by the toe kick. A finished panel is then glued and screwed to the cabinet backs (18).

upper cabinets. I marked the stud locations on the hanging strip of the first upper cabinet and drilled holes through to the inside of the cabinet (photo 19, facing page).

Next I cut two 2x riser blocks to the exact distance between the upper cabinets and lower cabinets. I screwed the blocks to the wall where the screw holes would be hidden by the backsplash (photo 20), which let the

base cabinets take the weight and set the level. I then placed the predrilled cabinet on the blocks and pushed it into place against the wall.

I drove screws through a couple of the holes to hold the cabinet in place temporarily while I checked for plumb and level. Shims were added where needed, and then I drove in permanent screws through all the

Upper Cabinets Get a Boost

Stud locations are marked on the back of the cabinet, and holes are drilled (19). Blocks cut to the distance between the uppers and lowers and screwed to the wall (20) hold and level the cabinet until screws are driven into the predrilled holes (21). After plumbing and shimming are done, extra screws are driven through the hanging strip and through the face frame.

predrilled holes (photo 21). I also predrilled and drove in screws along the bottom inside of the cabinet and through the face frames.

I rechecked the corner cabinet for plumb and followed the same installation procedure for the rest of the uppers. At the window, I set the wall cabinet to the right of the window and then scribed the left-hand cabinet so that it fit at the same distance from the window.

Finishing Up

As the upper cabinets go in, I pay extra attention to the doors to make sure that plumbing and leveling haven't caused them to rack. If I do notice a racked door, I try to cheat the cabinet a little to compensate, or I fine-tune the door after all the cabinets are

in. I finish off the kitchen by applying the toekick, crown molding, and knobs.

These kitchen cabinets came with holes for the knobs already drilled. But if this isn't the case, I double-check with the clients for the exact knob locations before mounting the knobs or pulls. I putty all the nail and trim-screw holes, but usually save any touchup until after the countertops are installed. All doors are given a last check for swing and fit, and I check shelves, drawers, lazy Susans, etc.

I give the room a quick sweep, which keeps me in the good graces of the clients and contractors and ensures that I've rounded up all my tools. Now we're finished. Let's eat!

Kevin Luddy runs Keltic Woodworking, a custom-carpentry and cabinet-work business in Wellfleet, Massachusetts.

Simple Frameless Cabinets Built on Site

■ BY JOSEPH B. LANZA

I have to admit I was a bit slow to catch on to the advantages of frameless cabinets. I had problems with the edgebanding and the European-style cup hinges that inevitably go along with frameless cabinets. When I first tried the hinges, I found them awkward to use. Setup and layout meant deciphering arcane diagrams with odd, unfamiliar dimensions. The much-touted adjustability of the hinges seemed to require an awful lot of adjusting and readjusting. Frustrated, I concluded that this cabinet-hinge combination was best suited for factory production or, at the very least, a shop dedicated to the 32mm cabinetmaking system that originated in Europe.

But that was quite a few years ago. Now, after a series of improvements to both the hardware and the user, I find myself using these hinges all the time. The clip-style hinge, now made by several manufacturers, is a big improvement over earlier versions. This hinge makes it possible to hang and remove doors quickly, without tedious readjustment every time. I incorporated these hinges into a hybrid system for building face-frame cabinets with inset doors.

These hinges were so much better, they encouraged me to give frameless cabinets another try. They have a clean look that seems especially well suited to a spare architectural style. I looked for a way to build them on site quickly and easily, and the answer was simple: Make cabinet boxes just as I'd been making drawer boxes for years.

Using Baltic-Birch Plywood Eliminates Edgebanding

For the little guy, edgebanding has always been the biggest headache in building frameless cabinets. The commonly available iron-on edgebanding just doesn't cut it for me, and ripping, applying, trimming, and sanding thin strips of solid stock is a huge pain in the neck. Because I make most of my drawers from ½-in. Baltic-birch plywood with tongue-and-groove corner joints, I realized I could

make cabinet boxes the same way with ¾-in. stock. Unlike ordinary hardwood plywood, Baltic birch is all birch with no softwood and no voids in the core. It is made up of thin veneers of alternating grain, which makes for a pleasing striped pattern when the edges are sanded or routed. Edgebanding can be avoided entirely.

As with cup hinges, Baltic birch can take a bit of getting used to. It comes in 5-ft. by 5-ft. sheets, so if you don't have long arms, a plastic panel lift will come in handy. Baltic birch tends to warp if left unused and un-braced, so if it looks as if it has been around

the lumberyard for a while, you may want to pick from the middle of the stack. It also is notoriously out of square, so you will want to check for (or make) a straight edge before you rip it. The sheets also tend to vary a bit in thickness. I've never had a problem with sheets from the same lift, but I sometimes run into a mismatch when mix-ing leftover pieces with a new delivery.

That said, it is great, and I love to work with it. Here in Massachusetts, Baltic birch is stocked in quite a few lumberyards and at nearly all plywood suppliers. Prices for a sheet of ½-in. stock are around $25 and

A table-saw cutoff box ensures that cabinet parts will be square. When working with Baltic birch, don't assume that factory edges are square.

Strengthening a Tongue-and-Groove Joint

Orienting a cabinet bottom or shelf incorrectly (top) makes a weak joint. The shelf is susceptible to splitting and will behave as if it were the thickness of the tongue. Putting the joint together with the thick part of the shelf facing up (bottom) is the stronger option.

WEAK

Cabinet side

Cabinet bottom or shelf

Split

STRONG

Cabinet side

Cabinet bottom or shelf

about $35 for ¾ in., but you can usually get a substantial price break if you can buy a full lift.

Lay Out Cabinets on a Story Pole, Then Cut All the Parts

My first step in building cabinets always is to make a story pole, which is a piece of stock about 2 in. wide and as long as the longest dimension in the kitchen. I lay out everything on the pole. This procedure gives me a chance to make my mistakes at full scale and to check my measurements on site before building the cabinets. I mark all cabinet sides, tops and bottoms, and joints directly on the sticks. I make a cutlist from the stick, then rip and crosscut all the cabinet parts (photo, above) on a table saw.

Because there is no face frame to add strength and stiffness to the carcases, the corner joints have to be solid. There are a number of methods that work well— biscuits, screws, knockdown fasteners—but I like the tongue-and-groove joint. It is easy to set up on a table saw with a dado head, quick to cut and easy to assemble, and it gives lots of gluing surface. I make the cabinet sides full length and then cut the grooves in them, being sure to orient the groove so that the joint will have maximum strength (drawing, left). The cabinet tops and bottoms get the tongues.

The groove is ¼ in. wide and a strong ⅜ in. deep. I set up and cut all the grooves for the base cabinets at the same time. Then I move the fence 2 in. away from the dado head and run the wall cabinet sides, which have a 2-in. gap at top and bottom (top left photo, facing page). These gaps lower the top shelf, allowing the cabinet sides to rise above it as a curb. This gap also makes room for the bottom rails that conceal the recessed lights.

The dado setup for the tongues is the same for all cabinets, so after I get a good fit

Grooving cabinet sides 2 in. from their bottoms creates space to hide over-the-counter lights.

When cutting the tongues, a featherboard attached to an auxiliary fence makes the process safer and the tongues more consistent in thickness.

on a test piece, I cut all of them (top right photo). To be strong, the joint must fit together snugly. Base cabinets don't have solid tops, just spreaders. To make them, I cut the tongue on a piece of scrap 6 in. to 7 in. wide (it's not critical), then rip that in half. These pieces go at the front and back of the cabinet to hold the sides together and to provide some support for the countertop. The cabinet bottom is, of course, solid. If the cabinets have backs, I cut them next (the cabinets in the photographs don't have backs). I make the cabinet rails from leftover ¾-in. stock.

Assembly Is Speedy with Screws or Air-Driven Nails

I assemble the cabinets with glue and, depending on what will be exposed, either screws or air-driven nails (bottom right photo). Because these base cabinets later received end panels, I used 16-ga. nails to assemble them and didn't worry about the holes. For the exposed sides of the wall cabinets, I used screws with integral washers. I used the same fasteners for the end panels and the exposed back of the kitchen island (photo, p. 55). I also used these fasteners to

Nails secure cabinet boxes while the glue dries. Check for square by comparing diagonal measurements before the glue sets.

attach aluminum trim throughout the rest of the house.

Cabinets without backs are checked for square after they are assembled, then laid on the floor until the glue sets. Before installing any of these cabinets, I ran a router with a ⅛-in. roundover bit around the inside and outside edges of the fronts. This little profile

After marking stud locations, the author hangs upper cabinets. Without backs and doors, these boxes are light enough for one person to hold in place as they are screwed to wall framing.

also fools the eye if the cabinets don't quite line up when they are installed.

I hung the wall cabinets first (photo, left) while they were easy to reach, then set the bases. Building cabinets in a lot of old, out-of-level, out-of-square houses has gotten me in the habit of building bases separate from the cabinets. I level the bases first (bottom right photo), then set the cabinets on them. I like to spray the exposed toekicks with black paint before the bases are installed. Then I set the cabinets (bottom left photo) and attach finished ends and backs.

I made drawers like cabinet boxes and installed them before cutting parts for the doors and drawer fronts. Both the drawer fronts and doors are slabs of ¾-in. Baltic birch.

To make leveling them easier, the author installs the bases separately from the cabinets. With the bases secured, he then sets the cabinet boxes in place and screws them to the wall.

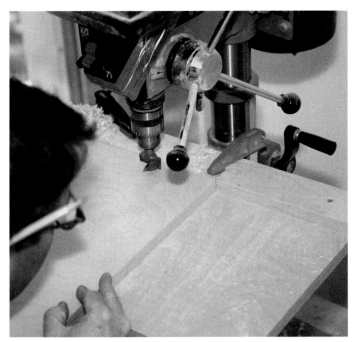

After testing the layout on scrap, the author drills 32mm holes in the backs of cabinet doors. Pencil marks on the drill-press fence indicate the door-edge alignment.

A jig locates screw holes for hinge plates inside the lower cabinets.

When it was time to drill big cup-hinge holes on the back sides of the doors, I set up a fence on my portable drill press. Pencil marks at 3½ in. on both sides of the bit space out the hinges equally (top left photo). I can drill one hole, slide the door across the fence until the edge reaches the other mark and drill the second hinge-cup hole. Before boring out a stack of doors, it is always a good idea to mock up a hinge on scrap stock to make sure that the layout is correct.

Before hanging doors, I ease the backs with a ⅛-in. roundover bit and the fronts with the ⅜-in. roundover to expose the edges of the birch plies. To hang doors, I made a plywood jig to drill holes for the hinge base plates (top right photo). When laid out correctly, the hinges snap easily together.

Joseph B. Lanza is a designer and builder who lives in Duxbury, Massachusetts.

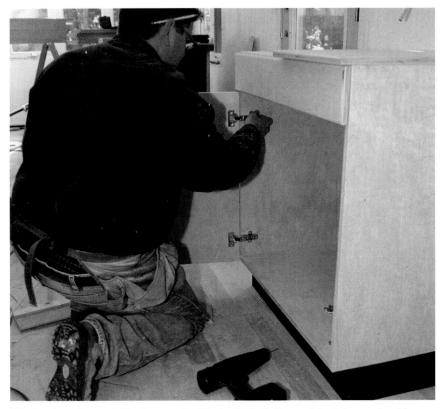

If holes have been drilled correctly, hinges installed on cabinet doors should snap easily into place on the base plates. These hinges allow the author to fine-tune the fit of the door.

Making a Solid-Surface Countertop

■ BY SVEN HANSON

Twenty years ago DuPont® introduced Corian®, the first solid-surface countertop material, to the building community. It was received with a chorus of yawns. On the one hand, it looked like stone but wasn't the real thing. On the other, it resembled plastic laminate while costing three to four times more money.

But this neither fish-nor-fowl quality of the material doesn't tell the whole story. The most desirable aspects of solid-surface material are its workability and durability. Unlike laminate, the color and pattern of solid-surface countertops go all the way through the material, which means it lasts longer and can be repaired easily. The material is almost as dense as stone—in the range of 100 lb. per cu. ft. But unlike stone, it can be glued up with imperceptible seams and cut and shaped with carbide woodworking tools. And as more colors and patterns have come on the market, the once-reluctant public has embraced solid-surface countertops in a big way.

Corian, which is made of acrylic plastic mixed with a powdered clay filler called aluminum trihydrate (ATH), now has competition. Other brands of solid-surface material, such as Avonite®, Surell® and Gibralter® (see Sources of supply), are made of polyester resin and the same ATH filler and color-fast pigments. The working properties of the materials, however, are the same. And even the distributors say that, once installed, the main difference between brands is pattern.

All of the manufacturers offer seminars on working with their material, and you typically need to take a course before you can buy the goods. That's because manufacturers are understandably nervous about bad fabrication practices infecting the reputation of their products.

When I started building solid-surface kitchens, I liked the patterns and colors of Avonite's materials. So three years ago I took their one-day certification class. It cost $50, most of which I made back in doughnuts, soft drinks, and router tricks.

Since that introduction to the material, I've made a lot of kitchen counters and lavatory tops, and I've taken Avonite's advanced

Once sanded and buffed, the seam (left of sink) is nearly invisible.

class. I've found the material to be surprisingly workable, and mistakes are pretty easy to fix, which is no small consideration when the material costs $15 per sq. ft. and up. This article is about the basics, and I'll focus on a typical kitchen counter to illustrate the tools and the techniques for working solid-surface materials.

Start at the Corner

Most counters have a dogleg in them where they turn a 90° inside corner—at least it looks like a 90° corner. Veteran installers have learned the hard way always to check for square and to adjust according to what's really there because solid-surface counters are tough to trim in the field.

If the counter's shape is complicated, I make a full-size template. I prefer ½-in. medium-density fiberboard (MDF) for template material, but cardboard will do in a

pinch. If you use cardboard, though, and need to collapse the template for transport, cut it into segments with a chevron or zigzag pattern; don't fold it. The segments can be reassembled only one way and won't lose the ¼ in. or more of length that folding can cause. If I'm replacing an old countertop, I sometimes use it as a template.

I start a job back in the shop by deciding the most efficient way to use the materials. Economy, maneuverability, and color matching all are important. For example, the project illustrated here had a 10-ft. long counter intersected by a shorter countertop (drawing, below). Avonite sheets are ½ in. or ¾ in. thick and come in 5-ft. or 10-ft. lengths that are either 30 in. or 36 in. wide. For a minimum order of 25 sheets, you can get ¼-in. thick material. I use ½-in. material for counters because it costs 30% less than ¾-in. thick stock. When supported every 18 in., it's plenty strong, and adding a built-up

---

Seams, Edges, and Corners

Like plywood, solid-surface material comes in wide panels that have to be ripped to the correct width. But unlike plywood, they can be assembled with nearly invisible seams. To build the L-shaped counter shown below, the author used three pieces. Because the counter was too unwieldy to preassemble, he made it in two sections that were then assembled on site.

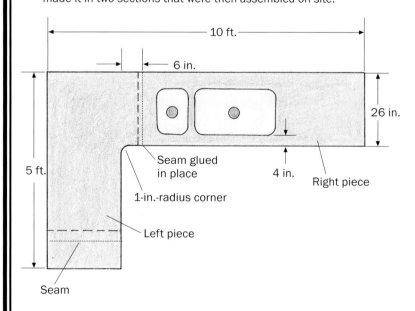

10 ft.

6 in.

26 in.

5 ft.

4 in.

Seam glued in place

1-in.-radius corner

Right piece

Left piece

Seam

BUILT-UP NOSING

The thick, rounded nosing of a solid-surface countertop is built up from ½-in. thick strips of the countertop material.

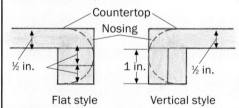

Countertop

Nosing

½ in.

1 in.

½ in.

Flat style

Vertical style

INSIDE CORNER BLOCK

Inside corners are radiused and reinforced with blocks.

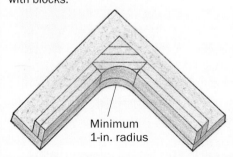

Minimum 1-in. radius

edge, or nosing, can easily make ½-in.-thick material look as though it's 1½ in. thick.

I bought a 10-footer and a 5-footer for this job, both 36 in. wide. The extra width costs more, but gives me matching material for backsplashes and built-up edges. I cut down the 10-ft. sheet to 85 in. (the right piece) and glued part of its offcut onto the 5-ft. sheet (the left piece) to make it the correct length. This way I made two manageable pieces by making an extra seam. I later joined the two pieces in place, making one L-shaped counter, but I'm getting ahead of the story.

Before making any cuts, I studied the color and pattern of the two sheets. Each batch of material is slightly different, so it's important to get sheets from the same run if they are going to be joined together. The pattern can even change from one end of the sheet to the other.

Ripping with Cornstarch

This counter is 26 in. wide, and with my first cut I ripped the 10-ft. piece down to 26½ in. (photo, above). Then I removed ½ in. from the other side to get rid of the factory edge, which is usually a bit rounded and sometimes chipped. Rather than fuss with the factory edge, I've found it more efficient just to eliminate it.

To minimize scratching, I saw the sheets face up, with a blade specially made for solid-surface materials (Golden Eagle Model G1060S). The blade's teeth have equally beveled top corners, resembling little coffins (this tooth configuration is called a triple-chip grind, or TCG). It makes a nearly chip-free cut on both top and bottom surfaces and works equally well on other plastics.

To help slide the unwieldy sheets across the saw, I dust the top of the table with cornstarch. Cornstarch is cheap, available, biodegradable, and won't contaminate the saw or the material.

Solid-surface materials come in big sheets that have to be ripped to width using a table saw with a special solid-surface blade. Sprinkling the saw's table with cornstarch makes it easier to slide the sheet. A dust mask is essential when working with the material.

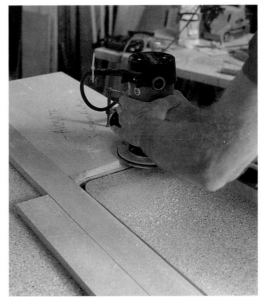

Inside corners have to be radiused to reduce stress. This MDF cutting guide has a radiused wood insert at its corner.

You shouldn't cut solid-surface material with a jigsaw. Its up-and-down action can cause fractures.

Next I lopped off the 10-ft. sheet to get a piece 85 in. long. I used a circular saw to make the rough cut, then jointed the edges with a router to get rid of the saw marks because each line in a saw kerf is a potential starting point for a stress-induced crack. Leaving the tooth marks voids the warranty on the material. By the way, you shouldn't cut solid-surface material with a jigsaw. Its up-and-down action can cause fractures.

A metal sleeve called a collar, or template guide, rides along the edge of the cutting guide and separates the guide from the ½-in. straight-flute bit.

A slot down the center of the mirror jig guides the router's collar as abutting pieces of counter are jointed simultaneously.

Note in the plan drawing of the counter that the inside corner is radiused (minimum 1 in.) and that the seam is 6 in. from the corner. These two details, which help relieve stress at the corner, require the left piece of the counter to look a little like an L. To cut the piece, I used a shop-built cutting guide (bottom photo, p. 63) that steers the router down the counter, around the corner, and off the narrow end where the joint will go. I use a ½-in. dia., two-flute bit to make this cut. A ¾-in. collar, or template guide, affixed to the router's base rides against the cutting guide (top left photo).

Solid-surface materials put heavy loads on a router and the bit. Manufacturers of solid-surface materials recommend 3-hp routers and bits with ½-in. shanks. I use the recommended ½-in. shanked bits, but my 1½-hp router has proven to be plenty powerful.

Joining Two Pieces

Inconspicuous seams between mating pieces are easy to make if the pieces fit together tightly. And the key to tight seams is the mirror jig (top right photo). My version is a

12-in. by 48-in. by ¾-in. scrap of veneered particleboard with a ¾-in. by 40-in. slot down the middle. I clamp abutting sections of counter to the jig, with their leading edges in correct alignment, so that my router bit cuts both their mating edges simultaneously. I support the pieces during the cut on a couple of 2x4s laid flat across a pair of sawhorses.

When I dry-fit pieces together, two tests determine a good seam. If a line can't be seen easily, I'm ready. If I see a gap, but the corner of a dollar bill won't fit into it, I'm still ready; otherwise, I must lightly recut the joint.

Before joining the pieces, I lay out marks for #20 clear plastic biscuit splines. Avonite is the only company I know of that requires them, but I use the biscuits no matter which brand of material I'm working with because the biscuits help align mating pieces. I place one 3 in. from each edge and add a third in the middle.

Using a square sanding block with 120-grit PSA (pressure-sensitive adhesive) sandpaper stuck to it, I give the edge, the top, and the underside of the seam two firm swipes each (top left photo, facing page).

Prior to glue-up, mating edges are cleaned up with a sanding block. This block is made with a sticky-backed disk stuck to a hunk of plywood.

Butt seams between mating pieces are aligned and strengthened with biscuit joints. Note the gray glue, custom mixed to match the material.

The possibilities of rounding the corners are outweighed by the probability that I'll knock down some extra plastic that might have held the seam open. Finally, I clean each edge and biscuit slot with a dust-free, colorless rag soaked with denatured alcohol.

Glue-Up

Before I mix a glue batch, I use hot-melt glue to attach 1x1 scraps to the face of the sheets on both sides of the seams about ½ in. from the edge. The scraps will supply clamping points for spring clamps. I use a medium-strength (clear or milky white) hot-melt glue, which can take plenty of spring-clamp pressure but can be peeled off without pulling up chips. The glue will usually lift away easily from the counter. If it needs coaxing, I pour some denatured alcohol on it and pry it off with a wide chisel.

Solid-surface glues come in two speeds: fast and slow. Both require a catalyst, and both have to be liquid to make a good seam. The fast glue has a pot life of about 7 to 10 minutes before it turns to marmalade. The glued-up pieces are ready to work in about an hour. Slow glue has a slightly

longer pot life of about 12 minutes, and pieces glued up with slow glue are ready to work in about eight hours.

The slow glue is a lot less expensive than the fast stuff. It's also more relaxing to use. I typically prepare all the pieces that need gluing, mix a big batch at the end of the day, assemble the parts and let them cure overnight.

Fast glues are available in different colors; you should use the one that matches the material at hand. For slow glues, I keep a range of Avonite glue pigments around so that I can mix colors as necessary. I go easy on the pigments because glues should be translucent, not opaque.

When I've got the color right, I stir in the recommended amount of catalyst. I've found that adding more catalyst just decreases the pot life of the glue without speeding the cure time.

Using a ⅛-in. bronze brazing rod, I shove glue into the biscuit slots and spread it along the edges. (I use brazing rods because they fit, and I have them handy.) Then I dunk the clear plastic biscuits (no wood, please) and stuff them into the slots (top right photo).

During glue-up, adjoining pieces are kept ⅛ in. apart while glue is drizzled into the gap (above). Then the pieces are put together, and spring clamps are applied on 3-in. centers to the 1x clamping blocks (right).

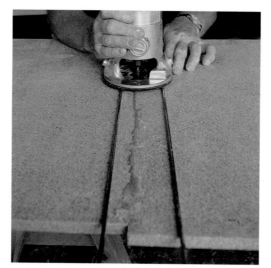

Cured glue squeeze-out is cut away with a straight-flute bit and a router riding on slippery tracks, such as these bronze brazing rods. The process is called skiing.

With the pieces on my 2x4 workbench, top-side up, I push them together within ⅛ in. and pour the rest of the glue into the gap. Then I align the front and back edges and apply the spring clamps to the clamping blocks every couple of inches. I should see a continuous bead of squeeze-out (top photos). Like epoxies, these glues must have

dimension. Too much pressure will cause a glue-starved seam, so spring clamps are the right choice for the job: They don't clamp so tightly as to squeeze out all of the glue. I let the squeeze-out cure rather than trying to remove it while it's still soft. Premature removal can lift the glue out of the joint.

I remove the cured squeeze-out with the router (photo, left). Called skiing, this method requires a router with a straight bit and a couple of thin runners for the router to ride on (I use bronze brazing rods).

When I've removed the glue from the bottom of the counter, I glue a seam block over the seam. Seam blocks are 4-in.-wide strips of the counter material that run the depth of the counter, minus any built-up edges.

Rounded Edges and Corner Blocks

A thick, rounded nosing on a solid-surface countertop gives the counter visual weight. To make the nosing, I rip two 1-in.-wide strips of edging stock from the cutoffs. Then

Built-up edges, or nosings, are formed out of two strips of Avonite. Here, a vertical strip is clamped to the counter's edge. Then a second strip is glued to its back.

As he rounds the inside corner, the author supports the router's custom base on edging strips. A dusting of cornstarch greases the track.

TIP

It's easier to adhere the edges with the counter upside down because you can see what's happening, and the glue stays in place.

with my sandpaper block, I lightly sand all faces, edges, and ends of the strips.

There are two ways to apply the edging. The best way is the vertical style (detail drawing, p. 62), but it requires very straight strips and smooth edges. If your table saw isn't up to that kind of a cut, the horizontal, or flat, built-up style will work better. I avoid the flat technique because it requires more glue, it squishes out of alignment when clamp pressure is applied, and it's more likely to have gaps between layers.

It's easier to adhere the edges with the counter upside down because you can see what's happening and the glue stays in place. I mix my glue, squeeze a bead along the edge of the outside strip, and clamp it in place. The strip should be either flush with the counter or slightly recessed—about $\frac{1}{32}$ in. An army of spring clamps on 3-in. centers applies the correct pressure. The second layer gets clamped to the first (top left photo). At inside corners, the edging

butts into reinforcing blocks (detail drawing, p. 62).

After the glue cures, I run my router against my inside corner guide to trim off any squeeze-out. Then I use the roundover bit to put the bullnose on the edging. I run the wide Lexan™ base of my big router on edging strips (lubed with cornstarch) to keep the bit steady and square to the work (top right photo).

As I mill the bullnose, I stop the router short of any butt joints that are still to come. This guarantees that I won't have a dip in the nosing caused by an inadvertent back cut. Before I flip the counter right-side up for bullnosing, I smooth the edge with my random-orbit sander running a disk of 60-micron paper.

After rounding over the top side in the same way as the bottom, I'm ready for some serious sanding. Although they are sanded at the factory, the sheets still need to be

Random-orbit sanding with 60-micron paper followed by 30-micron paper brings out the color and depth of solid-surface materials. A slurry of water with a few drops of liquid detergent speeds cutting and keeps down the dust.

A pipe clamp through each drain hole applies pressure. Wood blocks protect the sinks from the clamps, and the pressure must be light. Assorted other clamps hold down the edges to get even squeeze-out.

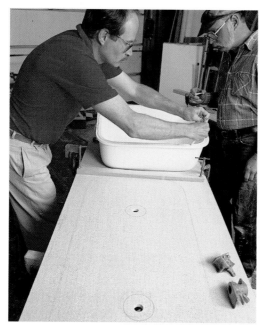

After drilling holes in the counter for pipe clamps, the author runs a bead of fast-set glue along the flange of the sink. The wood strip at its base will align the outer edge of the sink during glue-up.

buffed out. I start with 60-micron paper. I squirt some water and a few drops of liquid detergent onto the surface. This trick lets the paper cut faster, keeps the disk clean and suppresses dust (top left photo).

The Sink Top

Forget about those stupid little clips that come with some sinks to affix them to their counters. Solid-surface sinks are glued in place and become one with their work surface. I stuck two sinks under this counter.

To make sure the sinks ended up where I wanted them to, I made ¼-in. plywood templates that represented the sinks' outside perimeters and drain holes. I put the templates under the kitchen window and moved them back and forth until I liked the positioning. Then I noted the distance from the wall to the edge of the template.

I put the sink counter upside down on my 2x4 workbench. Then I transferred the sink measurements to the counter and marked the outlines of the templates with a pencil. The sinks are set back 4 in. from the front edge.

I drilled 1-in. holes in the countertop that correspond with the drain holes in the sinks (bottom photo, facing page). Then I mixed another batch of glue for the sinks. Once I had the glue spread and the sinks in place, I ran pipe clamps through the holes to exert some pressure on the assembly. Hand screws and spring clamps provided the rest of the clamping action (top right photo, facing page).

When the glue on the sinks cured, my colleague, Ed Schairer, and I gingerly flipped the still-tender, but very heavy, assembly and rested it on the 2x4s standing on edge. Then I got out my 2-in. by ½-in. flush-trimmer bit to remove the sink cutouts from the counter. I checked the bit's bearing to make sure it was firmly attached (you don't want it falling off during this operation), and I wrapped some vinyl tape around the bearing to keep it from marring the sink's surface.

From center hole I take the shortest route to the sink edge (photo, right). With the bearing pressed firmly to the side of sink, I cut clockwise. At the 3 o'clock and 9 o'clock positions, I stuck Avonite blocks with hot-melt glue to the sink cutouts. The blocks kept the cutouts from falling into the sinks as I finished the cuts. I used my roundover bit to radius the counter edge where it turns down into the sink, and I smoothed the transition with a random-orbit sander.

Counter Support

Solid-surface counters must be mounted on a lattice-type grid of supports 18-in. o. c. because plastics are natural insulators. A heat source like a toaster or electric frying pan will cause heat buildup, localized expansion, and stress. If the counter sits atop a solid base, such as a sheet of plywood, it won't get enough airflow around it to dissipate the heat. Solid substrates must be cut out to meet warranty requirements.

The old cabinets under this new counter needed a few 1x4s added on the flat to satisfy

The pipe-clamp hole becomes the starting point for cutting out the sink tops with a bearing-guided straight bit. The little blocks of Avonite were affixed with hot-melt glue to keep the cutouts from falling into the sinks.

the warranty requirements. The rule book also calls for continuous support under seams, so I put another 1x4 to the left of the sinks. I put vinyl tape on top of this support because a glued-in-place seam is above it. The glue does not stick to the tape. So the tape ensures that the top is not accidentally glued to the 1x4 support, which could eventually cause a crack to open up.

The supports also serve as anchorage for the counter. Thumb-size dabs of silicone caulk 18 in. o.c. are recommended. The counter squashes the dabs, making flat pads of stickum that can flex a little with the

Sources

Avonite®, Inc.
1945 So. Hwy. 304
Belen, NM 87002
(800) 428-6648

Corian®
DuPont®
P. O. Box 80010
Wilmington, DE 19880
(800) 426-7426

Fountainhead®
International Paper
Nevamar Div.
8339 Telegraph Rd.
Odenton, MD 21113
(410) 551-5000

Gibralter®
Ralph Wilson
Plastics Co.
600 General Bruce Dr.
Temple, TX 76504
(800) 433-3222

Surell ®
Formica®
10155 Reading Rd.
Cincinnati, OH 45241
(800) 367-6422

When the top has been sanded and buffed out, the two legs of the counter are joined in place atop the cabinets. Here the author checks the joint for closure.

counter. If you've got a one-piece counter, you can put the dabs down before you place the counter. This two-piece job called for a more complicated approach.

Gluing in Place

Ed and I wrangled the two counter pieces into position and dry-fit them to make sure the butt joint fit well. There is a ½-in. gap at both ends of the 10-ft. section between the wall and the counter. A backsplash typically hides the gap. For this job the slot in the brick veneer conceals it. The gap gave us enough room to slide the two pieces back a bit, then prop them up like a drawbridge.

I used hot-melt glue to stick clamping strips onto the sections. Then I mixed a batch of fast-set glue while Ed squeezed the silicone dabs onto the 1x4 supports. I dunked the biscuits in the glue, popped them in their slots and spread a bead of glue along the mating edges. Ed and I slowly low-

ered both counter sections, slipping the biscuits into the second section. I pulled the joint to within ⅛ in. and poured the rest of the glue into the gap. With front edges aligned, I jiggled the two sections together and applied the spring clamps (photo, left).

An hour later I skied down the joint to clean up the squeeze-out. Then I went against the manufacturer's recommendations and lightly sanded with the belt sander because the right piece of the countertop was a good deal higher than the left piece at the front edge. Avonite technologists think the unequal heating of belt sanding can cause stress damage to the seam, but two other manufacturers permit belt sanding, and I'm convinced that with a sharp belt and light touch to keep the material cool, there will be no problems. After applying water and detergent, I sanded the surrounding area and then touched it up with a Scotch-Brite® pad.

Manufacturers want to steer fabricator and homeowner to a 60-micron finish followed by a buffing with a Scotch-Brite pad. The resulting flat finish is easy to maintain and doesn't reveal flaws. It also doesn't reveal the beautiful depth in many of the patterns. My compromise is to put a little extra polish on with the 30-micron paper to make a punchier impression at the homeowner's first viewing, then knock it back a bit with a light buzzing with Scotch-Brite on the random-orbit sander.

Faucet cutouts are best done with a jig and a plunge router wearing a collar. But my client hadn't yet selected the faucet by the time I had to install the counter. Because there wasn't room to fit the router behind the sink once the counter was installed, I used a drill with a sharp spade bit to make the hole. Then I sanded out the drill kerfs with a little drill-mounted drum sander.

Sven Hanson ran a woodworking shop in New Mexico for 25 years. Now living in Italy and France, he takes new paths as they present themselves.

Adding a Backsplash

The client didn't want a backsplash for this job, but many situations will require it. For example, heavy-use areas such as sinks ought to have one. A backsplash keeps water from getting behind the countertop and makes the job look finished. It also offers a bonus to installers by giving them a gap of up to ½ in. along the wall for fitting the counter. Here's how I made a backsplash for another installation.

With a long straightedge as a guide, I use a router to joint enough material for the job, then I rip it to width. I precut it to fit exactly and then mark the butt joints onto their related pieces. Then I round over the top edge, stopping the router at the butt-joint mark.

When I like the fit, I put a fine bead of silicone caulk down the underside and arbitrarily place dabs of silicone on the back. Among them, typically at large gaps between the backsplash and the wall, I put globs of hot-melt glue. Within a minute of pressing a backsplash (down and in simultaneously), it is firmly stuck. If temperature changes move the backsplash, it can break the hot-melt glue bond and hang there with the flexible silicone.

If the wall is curved a bit, I place the backsplash piece in the sun. When the piece warms up, I flex it to the desired shape. Let cool. Install.

Counter backsplashes are attached to the wall with silicone caulk and hot-melt glue. The hot-melt glue holds the backsplash in place while the caulk sets up.

Making Concrete Countertops

■ BY THOMAS HUGHES

I was in the last stages of building a house for John and Kathy Buckley when they decided on a concrete countertop for their kitchen. Ordinarily when clients start making last-minute decisions like this, it can drive the builder to the aspirin jar. But I have to admit, my reaction was immediate and not even cautiously optimistic. I liked the idea.

John and Kathy considered marble and granite as a counter surface, but felt they were ostentatious. Plastic laminate lacked pizzazz. But concrete had just the right mix of a stark industrial image, weathered outdoor coarseness and coloration, and a sense of solidity and strength.

I've used concrete in many projects, from foundations to flatwork. So I felt comfortable with the task of forming the counters. The part of the project that I wasn't so sure about concerned the finishing of the counter to a surface that would be tough enough to withstand kitchen usage.

First, Make Test Samples

Before beginning the actual counters, I made a series of 10-in.-sq. by 2-in.-thick concrete samples, using different finishing techniques on them. I used a magnesium float on some of the samples, which brought more cream to the surface. I steel troweled these samples, and they had a crackled look when they cured.

I let other samples cure without a steel-troweled finish. Then I sanded them with a belt sander and a random-orbit sander to reveal the pattern of sand and aggregate. I applied the finish I had chosen for the counter (more on that later) to the samples and had the Buckleys evaluate them. They chose the most uniformly gray of the steel-troweled batch, with a little aggregate showing from sanding for color and texture.

All three of us liked the somewhat honeycombed edges of the sample blocks. The edges were marked with the typical voids and cavities of poured concrete, where lumpy clusters of cement-coated pebbles reveal the rocky contents.

A Two-Piece Countertop

Where to pour? That's the dilemma facing anybody who's making a concrete countertop. If you cast the top in place, you elimi-

A thin, gray line reveals the seam. Cast in two sections, this L-shaped concrete countertop is joined at the inside corner. The two sections are held together by joint connectors and epoxy. A tough finish of moisture-cured urethane protects the countertop from spills.

nate the hassle of moving around a heavy, cumbersome slab of concrete. But there are problems with that approach. In addition to dealing with the mess that accompanies any concrete pour, a countertop has to be etched with muriatic acid and then thoroughly rinsed before its finish can be applied. I didn't want to introduce that wild card into the final stages of trimming out the Buckleys' house.

In this case, I made the top in the garage, which meant that I could slop concrete around without worrying about the floors and the walls. Then I could take the top outside to rinse it off.

The kitchen base cabinets were L-shaped, with a 7-ft. wing and a 5-ft. wing. The countertops are 25 in. deep. Even with subtracting the sink cutout, the total weight would be around 500 lb. What's more, the awkwardness of moving such an odd shape out of the garage and up the stairs to the kitchen dictated splitting the top into two pieces.

Made of plastic-covered plywood and 2x sides, the forms were affixed to 2x4 handles for transport. In the background, the sink blockout is screwed to the form bottom.

A quartet of joint connectors was used to pull the two wings of the countertop together. The blocks glued to the form sides were removed after the pour, leaving slots for the connectors.

Build the Forms and Make the Joint

The bottoms of the forms for the countertop slabs were made from ¾-in. plywood. I cut the plywood 3 in. larger than the top in both directions to create flanges that support the form edges. I ran three 2x4s under each form as supports. The 2x4s extended beyond the form to serve as carrying handles (photo, left). I attached the plywood base to the 2x4s with drywall screws, making sure the heads were fully countersunk into the plywood. Then I stretched a layer of 6-mil polyethylene over the plywood and stapled it around the edges.

The countertop edges were formed with 2-in. tall strips that I ripped out of 2x stock. I beveled the tops of these strips to minimize the surface where concrete aggregate might collect as I filled the forms. I attached the form sides to the bottom of the form with drywall screws, but in this case I ran the screws from underneath, sandwiching the polyethylene between the plywood and the form sides.

People who make L-shaped counters out of particleboard and plastic laminate often use concealed joint connectors (photo, left) to draw the two pieces together evenly. I decided to apply the same strategy to this countertop, using Knape and Vogt #516 Tite Joint fasteners.

Joint connectors fit into holes that are typically drilled in the underside of the countertop. I avoided drilling by gluing eight ⅝-in. tall keyhole-shaped knockout blocks to the sides of the form. I beveled the blocks and sprayed them with WD-40 for easy removal.

To accommodate the 20-in. by 33-in. sink cutout, I made a block by screwing together two layers of ¾-in. plywood and another layer of ½-in. plywood. Then I screwed the block to the 7-ft. form from underneath (top photo).

Reinforce the Concrete and Strengthen the Mix

For strength during not only the life of the countertop but also during transport and installation, I decided to reinforce the countertop pieces with stucco wire. I also added polypropylene fibers to the concrete in the lower two-thirds of the countertop. I didn't use polypropylene for the entire mix because the fibers make it impossible to get a smooth finish on the concrete. Sold under a couple of trade names, these short fibers help reduce microscopic cracks in the concrete. I didn't need enough of the stuff to justify buying a minimum order. Fortunately, my local concrete supplier keeps the fibers on hand and was kind enough to give me a small bag of them.

The narrow bands of concrete in front and behind the sink are potential weak points, so I reinforced them with ⅜-in. rebar.

Preparation for the pour included setting the forms onto leveled pairs of sawhorses so that there was no chance of ending up with a twisted countertop. Because it was handy and not as smelly as form-release oil, I used WD-40 as a release agent on the form sides.

I needed just a small amount of concrete for the countertops, so I used prepackaged concrete mix. Hoe in hand, I mixed the 3½ cu. ft. of concrete ⅔ cu. ft. at a time. As I mixed the batches, I added a handful of the polypropylene fibers. I also added enough extra portland cement to bring the concrete to a six-sack ratio, which increased the concrete's compressive strength.

I screeded the concrete to the tops of the forms, then I smoothed it first with a wood float, then with a magnesium float. After the tops had set up for about three hours, they were ready to be steel troweled (photo, above). The concrete should be hard enough that pushing on it with your finger doesn't leave a depression, but you

After screeding the concrete into the forms and tooling the surface with a magnesium float, the author leans into the final finish of the countertop with a steel trowel. He then wrapped the counter sections in plastic and left them to cure for two weeks.

can still compress the top layer of fines (the creamy cement and sand mixture that rises to the surface during troweling) by applying hard pressure with the trowel. You can't be timid about troweling. You really have to lean on it. After troweling, I let the slabs cure for a day.

The next day I removed the form sides, leaving behind the knockout blocks for the joint connectors, and lightly sanded the edges with 100-grit wet-dry paper. That gave me the slightly rounded edges I wanted. Then I wrapped the countertops in plastic and let them cure for 2½ weeks.

Install the Countertops

A few days before I installed the countertop, I wet-dry sanded the entire top to 120 grit. Besides hand sanding, I also found the random-orbit sander, fitted with silicon-carbide paper, to be effective, although not particularly economical with regards to the life of a disk of paper. On the advice of the tile and masonry contractor, Nikos Maragos—a native of Greece who started out doing terrazzo floors—I mixed up a paste of portland cement and acrylic additive for tile work and squeegeed it over the tops to fill

The author grinds the joint flush with a random-orbit sander. Next he'll fill what tiny crevices remain with a paste of acrylic admixture and portland cement.

After sliding the countertops onto their cabinet bases, I test-joined the two tops. Then I loosened the joint, applied epoxy to the joint faces, and drew the joint tight again for a permanent bond.

I drilled a half-dozen pilot holes with a masonry bit through the plywood sub-counter into the concrete countertops and affixed them with 1¼-in. concrete screws. Finally, I filled the seam gap with a paste of cement and acrylic admixture. When it set up, I smoothed the joint with my random-orbit sander (photo, left), and seeing it was about midnight, called it a day.

The countertop pieces were now united into a monolithic unit and firmly anchored to the base cabinets. The fragile, thin sections of concrete that border the sink were thoroughly supported from below, so with the help of my jigsaw, I removed the block of plywood that located the sink opening (photo, facing page).

A Tough Finish of Moisture-Cured Urethane

The finish recommended to me was a moisture-curing aliphatic urethane called Wasser MC-Clear. This is an industrial-strength coating used primarily to protect bridges. It's often applied to concrete structures to protect them from graffiti. Unlike typical finishes, this finish cures faster with higher humidity.

Instructions for a usable surface called for two coats thinned with a proprietary thinner. You can apply the coating with a brush or a roller. I used a brush, and I found that the bristle lines from brushing leveled out quickly, leaving a very smooth, polished surface.

Moisture-cured urethanes contain iso-cyanates. You can protect yourself while using them by wearing a respirator fitted with an organic-vapor cartridge, but only if you're monitoring the vapors to make sure

any small voids. Then I sanded the tops again to remove excess filler.

I moved the tops outside, washed them with a diluted solution of muriatic acid and rinsed them with water, as called for in the finish instructions. After the countertops dried, I enlisted the help of my two working buddies, Scott Rekate and Knox Swanson, and we moved the tops to the kitchen for installation.

The maple cabinet bases, 1¼ in. shorter than standard height to accommodate the 2-in.-thick countertops, were already in-stalled. I drilled holes in the plywood sub-counter to gain access to the joint connectors.

By setting up the forms even with the cabinet tops, the countertops could be moved right into place. I slid each top off its form so that I could reach under the ends where I'd placed the knockouts for the joint connectors. I extracted the knockout blocks from below by running a screw into each one and then pulling on the screw.

Once the countertop was safely in place atop the base cabinets, the sink blockout could be removed. The author cuts out the bulk of the plywood block by drilling holes near the corners and then connecting them with a jigsaw. The remaining plywood edges are then carefully peeled away from the concrete.

Sources

The Glaze 'N Seal Co.
18207 E. McDurmott #C
Irvine, CA 92614
(949) 250-9104
www.glaze-n-seal.com

**Knape and
Vogt Mfg. Co.**
2700 Oak Industrial
Dr., NE
Grand Rapids, MI
49505
(616) 459-3311
www.knapeandvogt.com

**OSI Sealants Inc.
(formerly
Darworth Co.)**
7405 Production Dr.
Mentor, OH 44060
(800) 321-3578
www.osisealants.com

**Wasser High-Tech
Coatings, Inc.**
1004 W James St.
Kent, WA 98032
(800) 627-2968
www.wassercoatings.com

they stay below recommended levels. To be safe, you should wear a supplied-air respirator. Adequate ventilation is therefore an absolute must, and you should make sure there aren't any ignition sources in the area.

There are more user-friendly concrete sealers on the market, but I haven't tried any of them. My concrete supplier recommends waterborne acrylic sealers. They aren't as durable as moisture-cured urethanes, but they can be renewed periodically with minimal effort. The Glaze 'N Seal Company sells both water-based and solvent-based concrete sealers that can last 8 to 10 years when used indoors.

Framed by a Splash of Copper

To cap off the elemental feel of the countertops, I ran a 4-in.-high backsplash of ⅜-in.-thick copper around the edges of the coun-

tertop where it meets the wall. Before installing the copper, I washed it a couple of times with a muriatic-acid wash. Then I left the copper outside for a week in our salty winter weather. Once the patina looked right, I finished the copper with two coats of D-18 from Ultra Coatings to preserve the coloration.

Countersunk brass screws affix the splash to the wall. Where the copper meets the concrete, I sealed the joint with clear Poly-seamseal® caulk from the Darworth Co. The plumber didn't have any problems installing the cast-iron sink, but he did have to fasten the dishwasher to concrete, rather than to the usual wood.

Thomas Hughes builds houses and makes furniture on the northern Oregon coast.

Making Plastic-Laminate Countertops

■ BY HERRICK KIMBALL

As a carpenter's helper I learned the basics of working with plastic laminate 22 years ago. Since then I've fabricated more countertops than I can remember. Over the years I've witnessed a lot of mistakes and have made a few of my own. But there was a lesson in every error, and I've learned my lessons well. The tools and the techniques I'll describe in this article make it easier and less frustrating to fabricate professional-quality countertops.

It's Not All Formica

Among the general public, all plastic laminate is commonly referred to by the brand name Formica. In fact, many customers don't understand what I'm talking about unless I use the phrase "Formica countertop." The confusion is understandable considering that the first plastic laminate was, indeed, Formica, but now there are other manufacturers. Most of my tops are done using Wilsonart® laminate, but there is no difference between working with one brand or another.

Plastic laminate is made by bonding multiple layers of resin-impregnated kraft paper under heat and high pressure. The sandwich is topped with a colorful layer of melamine.

Several manufacturers also produce a solid-color, or solid-core, laminate. This product is uniformly colored throughout its composition, so the dark band that shows up on the edge seams of standard laminate is eliminated. Another solid-core selling point is its ability to hide scratches that would show up on standard laminate.

I seldom use solid-core laminate, though. It's more expensive, comes in fewer styles and, frankly, my customers expect a dark seam line on a laminate counter. If you use solid-core laminate, you should know that it's worked like regular laminate, but it's more brittle.

Aside from the myriad choices of colors and patterns available, there are also different types of laminate, such as fire rated and chemical resistant. But if you go to your local lumberyard and order a sheet of, say, Erin Glenn #4627-8, the salespeople are going to assume you want the standard, general-purpose laminate, which is what I use on virtually every residential and light-commercial countertop I make.

Sheets of plastic laminate come in nominal widths of 30 in., 36 in., 48 in., and 60 in. Nominal lengths are 72 in., 96 in., 120 in., and 144 in. The actual sheets measure 1 in. larger in width and length. Some manufacturers also offer 1¾-in. by 12-ft. strips of laminate for edgebanding.

Don't Scrimp When Estimating

On a small, straight-run countertop, figuring what size laminate you need is simple. But when you get into larger L- or U-shaped tops requiring one or more seams, estimating can be a challenge. Unfortunately, I don't know an easy way of doing this short of sketching out some laminate sizes and figuring each component of the countertop onto the sketched piece of laminate. There are things to keep in mind, though, when you do this.

First of all, even the best surface seams are unsightly, so avoid them whenever possible.

When a surface seam can't be avoided, I try to position the joint through a sink or a cooktop where it will be visible for only a couple of inches in the front and the back. Never seam through a peninsula or other high-visibility spot unless it can't be helped. Keep in mind also that any butt joints in the substrate should be placed as far away as possible from laminate seams.

When estimating laminate, allow at least ½ in. extra all the way around for finish trimming. Also, don't figure too close. If a 5-ft. by 8-ft. sheet will give you more breathing room than a 4-ft. by 8-ft. sheet when cutting out several pieces, get the extra, especially if you're new to the craft.

Low-tech, but effective. To cut laminate with a scoring tool, draw the tool across the laminate several times. Then, holding down one side, lift up on the other, and the laminate will snap cleanly along the score.

Tools for Cutting and Trimming

For years I roughed out all my laminate pieces with an inexpensive, carbide-tipped scoring tool. Using a straightedge to guide the cut, you draw the scoring tool over the top of the laminate (photo, above). This tool actually scrapes a groove through the surface. After a couple passes, hold the sheet down on one side of the line, lift up on the other, and the laminate will snap cleanly along the score. On long cuts, you start the snap at one end and work down the line.

Score-and-snap is an effective cutting technique, but it does have a couple drawbacks. It requires a large, smooth surface to lay the sheet on when cutting, and it's time-consuming.

Even the best surface seams are unsightly, so avoid them whenever possible.

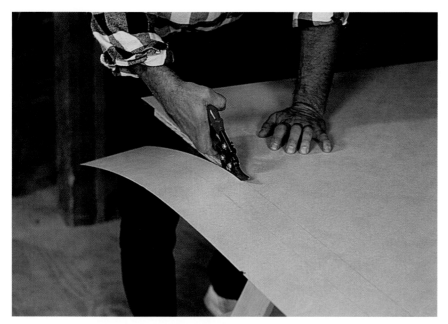

Shear force. Laminate shears, made by Klenk, have three blades—one above, two below—that remove a ⅛-in. strip of laminate. Cutting laminate with shears is faster and more convenient than cutting with a scoring tool.

Cutting strips with a slitter. Made by Virutex, this laminate slitter can either be pushed or pulled along a sheet. Its adjustable guide allows you to cut strips anywhere from ¼-in. to 3¼-in. wide.

> *If you're going to make more than a couple of tops, spring for a pair of laminate shears.*

Fortunately, I've discovered two tools that make cutting laminate sheets more of a snap than score-and-snap. The first is a pair of hand-held laminate shears (top left photo) from Klenk Industries, Inc. (www.klenktools.com). Similar in appearance to aviator tin snips, these shears have three blades, and together they remove a ⅛-in. strip of laminate. If you're going to make more than a couple of tops, spring for a pair of laminate shears.

But using shears can be tiring and time-consuming when you're cutting the long, thin strips needed for edging countertops and backsplashes. For these cuts, a table saw does a nice job—use a 60-tooth carbide-tipped blade, and make sure the sheet doesn't slip under the fence. A laminate slitter will do the same job without the noise, the dust, and the helper that the table saw requires. My slitter, made by Virutex (www.virutex.com), is hand-held and has two cutting wheels that shear a perfectly smooth line. The slitter is operated by pushing or pulling it along the sheet (top right photo), and an adjustable guide allows cuts from ¼ in. to 3¼ in. wide.

In addition to cutting laminate sheets to rough size, you also need to trim laminate after it's been glued to the substrate. Basically, trimming tools amount to a router and a bit, but there are choices here, too.

Any router can be used to trim laminate, but a 3-hp plunge router would be overkill. If you're going to deal with much plastic, it behooves you to get a small, lightweight laminate router (or trimmer). I like the Porter-Cable #7310 standard trimmer. At 5.6 amps, it's a powerful unit that I can hold in one hand and maneuver easily. It also has a rectangular base that comes in handy when cutting seams (more on this later).

Laminate-trimming router bits are made to do one of two things: trim excess laminate flush and square to the surface it overhangs, or flush with a bevel at the top. Flush-and-bevel cutters come separately or as a combination bit. Laminate bits have carbide cutters and are guided by either a ball-bearing collar or a self-pilot bit.

When new, ball-bearing pilots work nicely. But after some hard use they can be a problem. I've had bearings stop rolling after being gummed up with contact cement. If the bearing seizes, it will spin with the cutter and burn a mark on the laminate. I'm ashamed to admit that I've burned more than one edge.

Bearing troubles led me to try a self-pilot bit. These cutters are milled out of a ¼-in. shank of solid carbide, and the pilot is an integral part of the bit; it spins with the cutter and rubs along the guide surface. You avoid burning by lubricating any laminate guide surfaces with a thin coating of petroleum jelly before trimming. Because self-pilot bits have less bulk than the bearing pilots, they work particularly well in small trimmers.

It's also possible to trim the laminate flush with a ¼-in. straight-cutting router bit if you have an auxiliary guide attachment for your router. This accessory works pretty well, but I don't use mine because the self-pilot bit is so simple and easy to use.

The 48-Hour Rule

With kraft paper as the raw material, plastic laminate is actually a wood product. In fact, a sheet of laminate is very similar to wood in that it has a grain direction, and it expands and contracts according to its moisture content.

Standards for dimensional stability of plastic laminate are set by the National Electrical Manufacturer's Association (NEMA), and they allow for 0.5% dimensional change with the grain and 0.9% across the grain. On a humidity range from 0% to 100%, that means a 5-ft. by 10-ft. sheet of laminate may vary in size by roughly ½ in. in each direction.

Dimensional instability will cause problems if the laminate and the substrate are not allowed to acclimate in the same environment where they'll be assembled. Forty-eight hours, with free air flow around all sides of the pieces, is the recommended conditioning period. An air temperature of 75° F with a relative humidity of 45% is ideal for conditioning, but this is not nearly as critical as the 48-hour rule.

When properly acclimated laminate and substrate are glued together, the two will expand and contract together without incident. What happens if the components aren't properly conditioned? Nothing, if you're lucky. I've found you can bend the 48-hour rule and get away with it, but bending too far makes unhappy faces all around. One common result of insufficient conditioning is that perfectly fitted surface seams will soon separate, and in some cases, edge seams will come apart.

Preparing the Substrate

Many of the old site-built countertops I tear out have a ¾-in. plywood underlayment, and there are still a few people around who think plywood makes a better substrate for laminate. But this is one instance where cheaper is actually better. I always glue my laminate to high-density particleboard. Sometimes called core board, this material is inexpensive and well suited for laminate work. Particleboard has a very uniform, flat surface and bonds to the laminate much better than plywood, which has an uneven, wavy grain pattern.

High-density particleboard comes in ½-in. and ¾-in. thicknesses and is sized for laminate work in 25-in. and 30-in. widths and in 8-ft., 10-ft., and 12-ft. lengths. It's also available in 4x8 sheets.

When possible, I take measurements on site, make complete countertops in my shop and then install the finished product. Not only is it easier and more convenient this way, but it also makes for less mess in the customer's home (which is no small matter).

A sheet of laminate is very similar to wood in that it has a grain direction, and it expands and contracts according to its moisture content.

Beefing up the substrate. With its flat, uniform surface, high-density particleboard works best as a substrate for laminate. But gluing and stapling strips of plywood under the edges (and the seams) of the particleboard makes a stronger countertop.

Sometimes, factors like size and shape or placement of a counter layout dictate that I make the top on site. If this is the case, and especially if the counter is particularly large, I can often fabricate the substrate in modular sections in my shop and then take them to the job site and finish the assembly.

My method of assembling the countertop underlayment is not the only way, but it's the best way I've found to make a durable substrate quickly and precisely. I use the double-layer approach: ¾-in., high-density particleboard on top and strips of ¾-in. underlayment plywood on the bottom (photo, above). I use plywood on the bottom because it holds fasteners better, it makes for considerably stronger overhangs and seam cleats, and if water spills over the front edge of the finished counter, plywood won't soak it up and swell like particleboard

does—a common problem in front of some kitchen sinks.

I rough out my particleboard top sheets approximately ½-in. oversize each way. After fastening the bottom strips, I'll cut the top to exact size. Because my standard countertops have a finished depth of 25 in. (which gives a 1-in. overhang over 24-in. deep cabinets), I buy 30-in. wide particleboard, rip off a 4-in. strip for the backsplash and have 26 in. left for the rough top.

I cut the plywood bottom strips 3-in. to 4-in. wide and fasten them around the perimeter of the underside with a liberal coating of yellow glue and 1¼-in. long, narrow crown staples in my pneumatic stapler. If you don't own a pneumatic stapler, use 1¼-in. coarse-thread drywall or particleboard screws. Using a Phillips bit in an electric drill, the screws will pull right through and below the surface of the plywood without a pilot hole or countersink. Whatever fastener you use, keep in mind that the rough top must soon be trimmed to exact size, and fasteners should be kept out of the anticipated cutline.

When fastening the plywood strips, I'm not concerned if they don't align exactly with the particleboard edges because I'll cut them flush later. It is important, though, that adjoining pieces fit tightly together. If there is a gap between abutting plywood pieces, the pilot on my laminate-trimmer bit will ride into the void and mess up the finished edge. When butting two pieces of particleboard together, I'll fasten a cleat underneath that spans the seam a minimum of 12 in. on each side. Peninsulas and islands often have eating areas that cantilever, and I always beef up these overhangs with a solid piece of plywood extended at least 12 in. back over the top of the cabinets. If a heavy sink is to be installed, I'll be sure to get extra plywood support there, too.

When the rough top is assembled, I cut it to finish size with a carbide-tipped blade in my circular saw and use a clamped straightedge as a guide. For long stretches, I have a 6-in. by 12-ft. length of particleboard that I use for a guide. If I can't get a regular clamp on this type of straightedge, I fasten it temporarily with screws. When cutting underlayment with the saw, watch out for screws used in assembly. Back the screws out if they're in your cutline.

It's essential that underlayment edges be cut perfectly square. If an edge is beveled in at the bottom, the guide bearing on the laminate bit will cut too close and shave the face of the laminate edge strip.

I cut the front edge and the back edge of the substrate first. Then before I cut the piece to length, I clamp the backsplash and the countertop together, edge-to-edge, and cut both at the same time.

I prefer to have sinks and cooktops in my shop and make all cutouts in the underlayment before I glue on the laminate. After the opening is cut, I'll drop the fixture in to check the fit. There is little hope for salvaging a botched cutout if the laminate is in place.

After the underlayment is trimmed to size, and just before gluing, I sweep the surface off with my hands. Fingertips will detect residual grit and surface imperfections the eye can't readily see. Surface imperfections need to be filled before gluing the laminate. Plastic auto-body filler dries quickly and works well. Instead of sandpaper, I use a block plane to knock off gobs of filler, dried glue, or uneven seam butts. I also double-check the edges and make a light cleanup pass or two there, if necessary.

Mirror-Cutting a Seam

If there is a surface seam to contend with, now is the time to match it up. It's impossible to achieve an invisible seam in plastic laminate, but if done properly, you can make a very tight seam that's not obvious.

The easiest way to make a tight seam is to mirror-cut the two abutting pieces of laminate with a router and a straightedge. To do this, I position laminate sheets on the substrate right where they will be glued down, with the two edges butted. Then I clamp the pieces so that they don't shift around and slide a scrap strip of laminate under the seam (top photo, p. 84).

Next I clamp a straightedge guide to one side so that it allows the router bit to cut down the center of the seam. With a ⅛-in. straight-cutting bit in my router, I set the depth to cut completely through the top layer of plastic and into but not through the scrap. I feed the router down the edge in one smooth, even stroke. Before unclamping the guide, I slide a square against it and pencil two index marks across the cutline. I unclamp the pieces of laminate, align the index marks, and I've got a perfect seam.

Cutting a seam. Although you should avoid seams in laminate whenever possible, sometimes you can't. Mirror-cutting is the way to get the best possible fit between two pieces. To do it, butt the pieces together temporarily and make a router cut through the middle of the seam.

Seize the spray. Although slightly more expensive than brushable-grade contact cement, spray cans offer advantages that make them worth the cost. Spraying means easier, faster application, quicker drying, and less fumes.

Before gluing, I scrape or file any burrs off the backside of the seam cuts, but I don't take any material off the face of the seam. If the edges don't meet as well as I'd like, I reset the straightedge and try again, provided, of course, that I can do so without making my pieces too short.

What a Difference a Spray Makes

Contact cement is the adhesive used to glue down plastic laminate. Until recently, small-time fabricators like myself have had to use brushable-grade cement that comes in quart or gallon cans. If you've ever glued a top using this stuff, you know all too well how noxious the fumes are. And if you've brushed, rolled, or squeegeed on as many gallons as I have, you've no doubt wished there was an easier, faster, cleaner way to get the job done. Well, there is.

Without a doubt, the best recommendation I can give on the subject of contact cement is this: spray it on (bottom photo). Production fabricators have used spray equipment for years to glue their tops, but only in the past couple of years have the advantages of spray been available to everyone in the form of aerosol cans.

I use 3M's Hi-Strength 90 spray adhesive (3M Adhesives Division, St. Paul, MN 55144; 800-364-3577) which I get from my laminate supplier. It comes in 24-oz. spray cans, and by my calculations, one container at 100% coverage will glue approximately 6 ft. of standard-depth counter, edge, and back-splash. Spray adhesive costs slightly more than brushable grade, but it's worth it. The spray is flammable, however, and while there are less fumes, they're still harmful, so be sure to have plenty of cross-ventilation when spraying.

To use contact cement, spray an even coating on both mating surfaces, allow the adhesive to dry, then bring the pieces together. When the glued surfaces touch, they stick. When they stick, they're stuck; there is no longer any chance for adjustment. A more permanent bond is made by applying pressure with a rubber laminate roller, or pounding a cloth-covered block of wood over the surface.

Laminate Meets Substrate

Edge strips go on first, and I always spray two coats of contact cement on the porous underlayment edges to ensure good coverage. Once the cement is dry on both the laminate and the substrate, bring them together. I start at one end and move across, centering the laminate on the substrate edge and pressing firmly as I go. With longer pieces, it's helpful to have someone support the other end of the strip while you work. On edges, I forego the cloth-covered block and apply pressure directly with a 16-oz. dead-blow mallet. Then I use a router with a flush-cutting trim bit to trim the ends and the top and bottom edges of the laminate flush with the substrate (top photo). It's important here to rout in the direction opposite the rotation of the router bit. If I'm standing in front of the counter, for instance, and trimming the top piece of laminate where it overhangs the front edge, I rout from left to right.

After all edges are glued and trimmed flush, I use a laminate file to remove minor milling marks left by the router bit. A laminate file is made specifically for plastic laminate and should be available from any supplier. Other files don't do the job. I hold the file flat against the countertop and make a couple of sweeps over the freshly routed edges, always filing toward the substrate. Don't file too much. Where edge strips meet at an outside corner, I first file the overlapping piece square, then bevel it slightly. I also run the file at a slight angle along the bottom to take off the sharp edge.

TIP

When gluing the laminate to the substrate, always make contact from the center out or from one end to another to avoid air bubbles.

Trimming the edges flush. A laminate trimmer is just a router that's been downsized to make it more maneuverable. Here, the edge strip on the front of the countertop is being trimmed flush with the top of the substrate.

Yes, those are Venetian-blind slats. As the name implies, contact cement sticks on contact, so you don't want two mating surfaces to touch until they're properly positioned. Venetian-blind slats work well to keep the laminate off the substrate until you're ready to start gluing.

It's not a ball-bearing bit. A ball-bearing bit can seize and burn the laminate. That's why the author prefers a self-pilot bit. To avoid burning, he lubricates the guide surfaces with petroleum jelly before routing.

Routing out for the sink. The author cuts sink and stove openings in the substrate before he glues on the laminate, which allows him to test the opening and make adjustments if it fits wrong. Afterward, it's a simple matter to knock a hole in the laminate and run the router around the opening.

With the edges glued, routed and filed, I spray the tops—substrate and laminate. To keep the laminate and the substrate from touching one another while I move the laminate into position, I lay salvaged Venetian-blind slats on the underlayment as temporary spacers (bottom photo, p. 85). After final positioning, I slide the strips out and press the laminate down as I go.

Always make contact from the center out or from one end to another. I once glued up a circular tabletop and made the mistake of pulling all my spacers out and pressing down the edges first. When I got to the middle I had a bubble, and the laminate didn't want to go down. Slightly panicked, I commenced to place extreme pressure on the trouble spot with block and hammer, and it stuck. I won the battle but not the war; a few days later the center popped loose.

The only way to break the adhesive bond and separate two pieces is with glue solvent. Use acetone or lacquer thinner. Mineral spirits will do the job, but it leaves a residue that will interfere with glue up next time around. Work a wide-blade putty knife under a spot on one edge and separate it just enough to spray a little solvent in the crack. Keep feeding the solvent in and pry upward as the bond dissolves. Be patient, let the solvent do the work, and you'll succeed.

When gluing two pieces that meet at a surface seam, stick one side down first, align the index marks, glue down the next piece starting at the seam and work away from there.

With the top piece glued into position and rolled or hammered down, it's time to trim the top flush (top left photo). Because I use a self-pilot bit, I spread a thin layer of petroleum jelly with my finger onto the laminate edge first. When cutting, always keep the router in motion when the self pilot is riding against the edge. If you have to stop, pull away from the countertop, or you may burn the edge.

To rout any openings in the top, I punch a hole just big enough for the trim bit to fit into, then I run the router around the opening with the self pilot riding against the opening cut in the substrate (bottom photo, facing page). Quick and easy.

Most stainless-steel sinks are held down with clips that fasten under the counter and require a ¾-in. thickness to grab onto. If my substrate is 1½ in. (double thickness) and is going to get a stainless-steel sink, I'll rout recesses for the clips at this time. Essentially, I just remove a section of the plywood layer in the spots where the sink clips will be positioned.

More Filing

Despite their name, flush-trim bits really don't cut perfectly flush. If you slide your fingernails up the front edge, they'll catch on the slight overhang. I remove this excess and finish off the edges by hand filing.

Some fabricators prefer to use a bevel-cutting bit, which can be adjusted to trim off the overhang and reduce filing time. I don't use a bevel bit anymore because it's a pain to adjust the height, and a bevel cut produces a wider, dark seam line that I find less desirable.

Filing isn't difficult, but it does require a careful touch. A sharp fine- or medium-cut laminate file is essential. I first remove the overhang by filing almost flat against the front edge (photo, above). Most of the cutting is done on the back half of the file in a forward-sawing stroke. You'll know you've gone exactly far enough when excess glue at the seam shaves off, revealing a crisp, clean edge. If in doubt, double-check with the fingernail test. After all the edges are finished in this manner, I ease the razor-sharp top corner down with a couple of light passes of the file (or sanding block), held at a slight angle. One thing you don't want to do is file inside corners square. The ¼-in. dia. radius left by the trim bit looks very nice and substantially reduces the possibility of stress-cracking in that area. Once you get the hang of it, filing can be done quickly and precisely.

Flush-trimming bits don't trim flush. You have to file the laminate top flush by holding the file almost flat to the front edge and stroking downward. You know you're done when the excess glue at the seam shaves off, revealing a crisp, clean edge.

I clean excess glue off the countertop with mineral spirits and a soft cloth. If I run into a difficult stain, I don't hesitate to use a little bit of mild abrasive cleanser (unless, of course, I'm working with a high-gloss laminate).

Attaching Backsplashes

Fastening countertops down is a straightforward job. The standard procedure is to drive screws up through cabinet corner braces and into the counter underlayment. This usually works best if a clearance hole is first drilled through the brace, and obviously, you want to make doubly sure the screws you use are long enough to grab well but not so long that they go through the top.

The backsplash. Clips hold a backsplash tightly to the countertop. Screwed to the back edge of the counter (photo, right), the clips engage a screw on the back of the backsplash. Once the counter is installed, the backsplash is snapped into place (photo, above).

Sources

Klenk Industries, Inc.
20 Germay Dr.
Wilmington, DE 19804
800-327-5619

**Virutex
(dist. by Rudolf Bass, Inc.)**
45 Halladay St.
Jersey City, NJ 07304
201-433-3800

Woodworker's Supply, Inc.
1108 N. Glenn Rd.
Casper, WY 82601
800-645-9292

Backsplashes are glued up just like countertops. I make up backsplashes as separate pieces and attach them after installing the countertop. Many fabricators glue their splashes in place with a bead of silicone, and they use no mechanical fasteners. I've used this approach too, but I've never felt right about it because I've seen backsplashes that have been installed this way separate from the counter.

I recently discovered some backsplash-attachment devices called Smart Clips in a tool catalog (Specialty Tools, 940 Lawhon Dr., Jacksonville, FL 32259; www.specialty-tools.com) and decided to try them. I wasn't disappointed; Smart Clips allow for quick, tight backsplash attachment. They're also relatively easy to use. The plastic clips are screwed down at least every 12 in. along the back of the counter. Aligned with the clips, drywall screws are driven into routed recesses in the backsplash (photos, above).

I run a bead of silicone along the bottom of the splash before snapping it into the clips. The clips have tapered slots that engage the drywall screws in the backsplash and pull the backsplash tightly to the counter. The only drawback to Smart Clips is their price: they're about 60¢ each, and the $50 installation kit is practically a necessity.

Fabricating a countertop is not difficult, but it does require a good measure of concentration and attention to detail. Mistakes can happen all too easily, and they are seldom as easy to correct. This fine line between success and failure is something that I find particularly appealing. Because of the challenges involved, nothing can beat the satisfaction that comes with a well-executed countertop.

Herrick Kimball is a remodeling contractor in Moravia, New York, and the author of Making Plastic Laminate Countertops, *published by The Taunton Press.*

Counter Act

■ BY STEVE MORRIS

People love laminate. If you took all the countertop laminate produced in the United States in a year—about 1.5 billion sq. ft.—you could pave Interstate 80 from New York to California and still put new kitchen counters in millions of homes.

Half of all countertop laminate is post-formed: It is heated and bent around a curved particleboard substrate to produce a seamless, counter-and-backsplash combination (sidebar pp. 94-95). Developed in the 1950s, postformed countertops are still a favorite among builders and homeowners. They are economical, widely available, and easy to install, even along undulating drywall. I must have fastened down a mile of postformed countertops last year, sometimes finishing two kitchens in one day. Along the way, I've learned some time-saving techniques to fit these factory-made surfaces to the waviest walls.

Measure at Least Twice

Standard countertops are 25½ in. deep and come in 6-ft. to 12-ft. lengths. With sections mitered together, postformed countertops conform to almost any cabinet layout. One rule about countertop joints, however: Keep them away from the sink. If water seeps into a joint, it can ruin the particleboard under-

A ready-to-install countertop. Postformed countertops are popular because of their integral backsplash and nosing. They can be cut and mitered at the factory and assembled on the job.

neath. Before measuring a kitchen for new counters, I sketch the plan view of the cabinets. I draw all the miters or butt joints, and mark any exposed ends of the countertop; they should overhang cabinets by ¾ in. If a stove or refrigerator fits between two cabinets, I leave a small gap on both sides.

Once the sketch is done, I measure each run of countertop along the front and back edges of the cabinets and take the larger

Measure the cabinets. You don't want to come up short, so measure the front and back of each section and take the largest dimension. If a countertop overhangs an end cabinet, add ¾ in.

Build up the tops of factory-made cabinets. To keep the postformed countertop flush with the top of the cabinets, you may need to add 2-in. wide strips to the tops of the cabinets. The strips are also used to fasten the top from below.

One rule about countertop joints: Keep them away from the sink.

of the two dimensions (left photo above). Layers of drywall tape and mud can build up as much as ¼ in. in the corners of walls. If you measure just along the wall, you may wind up with a top that is too short.

Unless by some miracle the walls are perfectly smooth and square, you will have to scribe the countertops to fit flush. Use a square or straightedge to see how wavy the walls are, and if extra material is needed, include this amount in your drawing.

Postformed countertops can be purchased any number of ways. At many home centers, you can buy premade blanks, which you cut yourself. Or you can have the home center or the countertop manufacturer do everything but install them, including join the miters. I usually have the factory do most of the countertop preparation. The integral backsplash makes cutting countertops with a circular saw a little tricky. The postforming factory and many home centers have special circular saws that make cutting postformed counters easy, so when possible, let the factory do the cutting.

The manufacturer will supply the end caps and end splashes, too. An end cap is simply a piece of laminate glued to the end of the countertop that covers the particleboard. An end splash is a laminate-covered piece of particleboard that continues the backsplash where a countertop butts up against a wall.

I stop short of having the manufacturer or the home center assemble the countertop joints. Although they can do a superb job, an L-shaped or U-shaped countertop is difficult to load into a vehicle and carry into a small kitchen. Also, preassembled countertops are more difficult to scribe and cut. I prefer to fit each piece of countertop separately and assemble the joints in place.

Prepare the Cabinets and Check the Fit

Postformed countertops have a ¾-in. or ⅝-in. strip glued along the front edge of the ¾-in. substrate, which makes the countertop look thicker than it actually is. The bottom of the strip should be flush with the top of the cabinets, not overhanging the face frame, which may mean you will have to build up the top of the cabinets. Do this before you lug the countertops into the kitchen and lay them on the cabinets. I usually fasten 2-in.-wide particleboard strips to the tops of the cabinets, perpendicular to the wall, with 1½-in. drywall screws (right photo, facing page).

With build-up strips in place, put the countertop on the cabinets and check the fit. If there are miters, see if the miter bolts will be accessible from inside the cabinets. (I sometimes have to cut an access hole to tighten the bolts.) If a U-shaped mitered section fits between three walls, you may have to trim the back corners with a belt sander to get the piece flush against the wall prior to scribing.

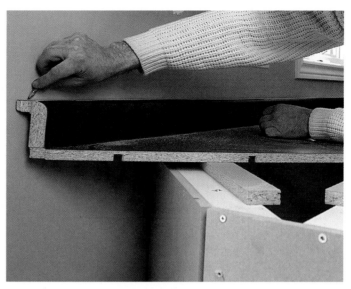

Scribe backsplash with a pencil and tape. If the gaps are small, run a pencil along the wall. For wider gaps, shim the pencil out the distance of the largest gap. Masking tape along the splash makes the line easy to see.

Scribing Is the Key to a Tight Fit

Almost all postformed countertops require scribing, or trimming, of the backsplash so that the backsplash will fit snugly against the kitchen wall. Even in many new homes, few walls are as truly straight as the backsplash on a postformed laminate countertop. Fortunately, the ¾-in. lip on the backsplash makes the chore of scribing an easy task.

I scribe the longest countertop first. With a piece of masking tape along the top of the backsplash, which allows me to see my scribe line, I push the countertop against the wall, making sure that I have a uniform overhang along the front edge of the cabinets. If I'm lucky, the largest gap between the backsplash and the wall will be just ¼ in. or less, although I have seen some gaps as large as ¾ in., even in newly built homes.

I use a pencil and a shim to scribe the backsplash, but you can use a compass or dividers, too. I start at the widest gap, shimming the pencil out just enough to touch the edge of the splash (photo, above). Hold-

ing the pencil-and-shim combination against the wall, I scribe the length of the backsplash. The line described by the pencil matches the wall's contour.

Bring on the Noise, Bring on the Dust

With the pencil scribe done, now comes the fun part, if you happen to have an itch for belt-sanding particleboard. First, I spin the countertop around so that the backsplash is at the front of the cabinets. Using padded clamps, I clamp both ends of the countertop to the cabinets and, with a belt sander and 30-grit sandpaper, I sand the particleboard back to my scribe line (top left photo, p. 92).

I recommend removing material slowly and beveling the substrate to make sure the top of the splash will come in contact with the wall. I also hold the belt sander so that the direction of the belt is parallel with the backsplash or slightly downward, toward the substrate. Otherwise, the spinning belt may chip the laminate. I always test-fit the piece as I scribe, checking the overhang to make sure I am not taking off too much. I

Belt-sand until it fits tight. To fit the backsplash to an undulating wall, use a belt sander with 30-grit sandpaper. Make sure the belt is spinning toward the substrate, and unlike this fellow, wear a dust mask.

Tighten miters at the front first. To assemble a miter, align the front edge and gently tighten the front bolt. Then insert a bolt in the rear mortise, line up the joint, and insert the remaining bolts.

Join miters with waterproof glue. Too much glue in a joint will swell the particleboard, leaving a bump in the surface of the countertop. Use just enough to produce a small amount of squeeze-out on top.

Tap the seam until you can't feel it. Before the glue sets up, align the top surface by tapping it with a hammer or a mallet until you barely feel the seam. Then tighten the bolts from underneath, and let the joint dry before moving it.

also check the miters; scribing changes how one piece fits with another.

Belt-sanding is a tedious task, but with patience, you can mate the backsplash flush to the wall. Although I don't always follow my own advice, wear a dust mask and hearing protection; there's no need to sacrifice your health for the sake of a well-fitted countertop.

Make the Miters Disappear

When all the countertops sit flat against the wall and tight to each other, I'm ready to assemble the miters. Small pieces can be assembled on the floor or bench. For longer counters, it's better to join the miters in place. (Large countertops may not fit into

A finished miter is nearly unbreakable. Glued and bolted, a miter joint is as strong or stronger than the surrounding particleboard. Still, it is a good idea to wait for the glue to set before moving or fastening sections of countertop.

Don't pierce the top after all that work. Use 1¼-in. #8 wood screws to fasten the countertop to the cabinets and to the 2-in.-wide strips applied along the tops of the cabinets.

the kitchen or bathroom after they are assembled.)

The miters are glued and bolted (some people also use biscuits or splines, but I don't). First, I spread a bead of waterproof yellow glue on the joint (bottom left photo, facing page). If the joint is closer than 12 in. to a sink, I use epoxy. Be frugal with the glue; if you use too much, the particleboard will swell, forming a bump on the surface.

With the glue spread, I place the mating pieces together and insert a bolt into the slot closest to the front edge, tightening the bolt just enough to hold the pieces (top right photo, facing page). As I draw the front edge into alignment, I place another bolt in the rear slot and align the back edge (don't worry about aligning the top yet). The backsplashes may not align perfectly; if this happens, leave the error at the back.

Insert and gently tighten the remaining bolts the same way. Before tightening the bolts completely, align the top with a hammer or rubber mallet (bottom right photo, facing page) until you can barely feel the seam. When the joint is smooth, tighten the

The sink is the last step. With the template supplied by the sink manufacturer, cut the sink opening in the countertop. To prevent an accidental scratch, the author attaches cardboard to the base of his jigsaw for cutting the hole for the sink.

Seven Steps to a Seamless Surface

Postforming a countertop for a kitchen takes a matter of minutes, as Steve Morris and I discovered when we visited Formatop in New Hamburg, Ontario, to see our burgundy countertops being made.

The process began at a roaring machine composed of sawblades and routers. It cuts sheets of particleboard, glues on the scraps to build up the edges, and then shapes the backsplash and nosing—all in one deafening step (photo 1). After both the particleboard and laminate were sprayed with contact cement and sandwiched together (photo 2), they were sent into the postformer. The postformer uses heat and pressure to wrap the laminate over the rounded edges. It also cuts the backsplash and bends it vertically, gluing a strip on the underside to hold the backsplash in place (photo 3).

With the postforming complete, Steve and I drove the blanks to Beaver Lumber in Sarnia, Ontario, where the countertops were cut to length and mitered with a stationary circular saw (photo 4). Mortises for the miter bolts were routed into the particleboard (photo 5), and thin strips of wood were used to build up the ends of the countertops for the end caps (photo 6). The end caps (pieces of laminate that cover the exposed ends of the countertop) were applied with sprayed-on contact cement. A laminate trimmer and flush-cutting bit were then used to trim off the excess (photo 7). Finally, a flat file smoothed the rough edge left by the laminate trimmer, and the countertops were ready to be installed.

Zachary Gaulkin is a former associate editor at Fine Homebuilding.

This is plastic laminate's Achilles' heel: Once broken or damaged, there is no way to repair it.

Fit to perfection. With careful scribing and installation, you can fit a countertop flush with the surrounding walls and make the miters disappear.

bolts, and then pin the mating backsplashes with a finishing nail through the particle-board strip that goes behind the backsplash.

Use Caulk Sparingly; It's Not a Piece of Trim

After the glue dries, I fasten the counter onto the cabinets with 1¼-in. #8 wood screws at the front and back, every 2 ft. or so along the length of the countertop. Be careful—it's easy to pop a screw through the laminate. (Some cheaper countertops may be thinner than 1½ in., requiring shorter screws.) If a screw pushes up on the laminate but does not pierce the surface, slowly back it out and tap the laminate flat. If you break it, you're out of luck. This is plastic

laminate's Achilles' heel: Once broken or damaged, there is no way to repair it.

With the countertop secured, I check for gaps along the backsplash. If I've done my scribing right, there should be no more than a hairline between the backsplash and the wall. A tight seam will not stop water from trickling behind the countertop, so it's wise to caulk the backsplash near the sink. I cut the minimum off the plastic tip of the sili-cone-caulk tube for a narrow bead.

Steve Morris is a finish carpenter, cabinet maker, and counter fabricator and installer in Sarnia, Ontario, Canada.

Tiling a Kitchen Counter

■ BY DENNIS HOURANY

It took two days to complete my first shower, including the time I spent at the library reading up on how to do it. That was 26 years ago. Since then, I've laid hundreds of tile floors and counters. My San Francisco-area tile-contracting company often works in housing develop-

ments where a journeyman tilesetter with only one helper can set a tile counter in a single day. Even if you don't set as much tile as we do, installing a kitchen counter should be a straightforward and relatively speedy process.

A Tile Counter Built to Last

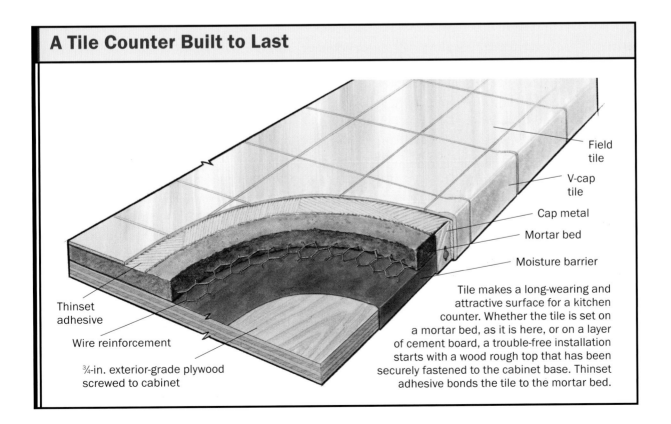

Field tile

V-cap tile

Cap metal

Mortar bed

Moisture barrier

Thinset adhesive

Wire reinforcement

¾-in. exterior-grade plywood screwed to cabinet

Tile makes a long-wearing and attractive surface for a kitchen counter. Whether the tile is set on a mortar bed, as it is here, or on a layer of cement board, a trouble-free installation starts with a wood rough top that has been securely fastened to the cabinet base. Thinset adhesive bonds the tile to the mortar bed.

Don't get hung up on the substrate. Dennis Hourany starts a tiled kitchen counter with a mortar bed (left photo), but you don't have to. Cement board (right photo) is another choice. For more on cement board, see the sidebar on p. 106.

Tile can be set on either a mortar bed or a cement board (photos, above). Around here, counters are almost always set on a mortar bed ¾ in. thick. I think that produces the best tile job—it's strong, durable, and easily leveled. Whichever substrate you choose, the process of laying out the counter and installing the tile is identical.

Before you put down either cement board or a mortar bed, make sure you have a solid wood base on top of the cabinets. I use a ¾-in. exterior-grade plywood (although you can also use 1x6 boards with ¼-in. gaps between them). If you use plywood, it's a good idea to make a series of cuts through the sheet with a circular saw to prevent the rough top from warping. Snap a series of parallel lines 6 in. to 8 in. apart along the length of the plywood, then make 6-in. to 8-in. long cuts along the lines, leaving 6 in. to 8 in. between them. Where overhangs are larger than about 8 in., you must provide adequate support—with corbels, for example—to prevent movement in the plywood that would crack the tile or grout.

Protect Cabinets from Moisture

Mortar is wet stuff, so we install a moisture barrier over the rough top of the cabinet. You may use an asphalt-impregnated paper such as 30-30 kraft paper, 15-lb. roofing felt or 4-mil polyethylene film. When we staple the material to the rough top, we let it hang all the way to the floor to protect the cabinets as we install tile. Excess paper can be trimmed away later. Paper should cover all rough-top edges, including those around the sink cutout and any other openings. Seams should be lapped at least 2 in. If you are installing backsplash tiles over a mortar bed, extend the paper up the wall beyond where the tile will end to protect the wall. Or use masking tape to protect untiled areas of the wall above the backsplash.

A mortar bed should be reinforced with some kind of metal lath. The kind approved by the Tile Council of America℠ is a galvanized, expanded type that should weigh at least 2½ lb. per sq. yd. We use 1-in., 20-ga. galvanized stucco netting or chicken wire. I like to run the wire on the deck and up the wall to within ½ in. of where the tile will stop, provided the backsplash tile does not extend up the wall more than roughly 8 in. If your plan is to carry the tile all the way to the bottom of the upper cabinets, then cut the wire at the juncture between the deck and the backsplash and install a separate piece of wire on the wall.

We staple the wire every 4 in. to 6 in. with staples at least ⅜ in. long. After the wire comes cap metal, which supports the perimeter of the mortar bed and is used as a guide to screed the surface (bottom left photo, facing page). Cap metal comes in a

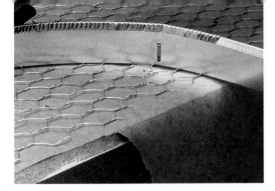

Getting the kinks out. To avoid kinks in the cap metal where it goes around a curve in the counter's edge, make a series of cuts in the top edge at the bend with a pair of aviation snips.

Level the metal. Once the cap metal has been leveled, Grijalva drives the nails home. By keeping the top edge of the cap metal ¾ in. above the top, he knows the counter will be thick enough at any point.

Cap metal supports the mortar. Elite Tile's Ernie Grijalva loosely nails cap metal to the edge of a counter. Moisture-resistant asphalt-impregnated kraft paper protects the plywood.

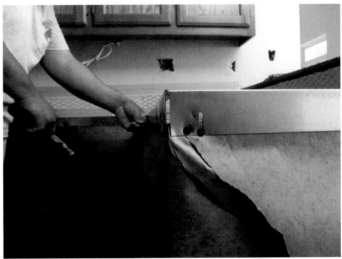

A second nail for insurance. Slots in the cap metal allow it to be adjusted up and down for level. Once leveled, the cap metal is anchored with a second nail driven right through the metal.

variety of shapes and sizes. We typically finish counter edges with a piece of tile called V-cap, which forms a 90° tile corner, so our cap metal is usually the J-cap variety. You can get cap metal at tile-supply houses or at some of the super hardware stores.

One big advantage of a mortar bed is that you can provide a level surface for tile even if the cabinets are not quite level—something that's harder to do when you're using cement board. So make sure the top edge of the cap metal is level before you are snugging up the nails and fixing the cap in place (photos, right).

Two Kinds of Mortar Make a Bed That Can Be Tiled the Same Day

We use two types of mortar in a counter: fat mud and deck mud. Because it contains lime, fat mud is sticky enough to adhere to vertical surfaces. For most horizontal surfaces, we use deck mud, a much drier mix that is not as susceptible to shrinking or cracking.

Fat mud (no, I'm not sure how it got its name) is a mixture of 5 parts plaster sand, one part portland cement and one part

Deck mud is a dry mix. Add just enough water so that the mortar holds its shape when it is compressed into a ball.

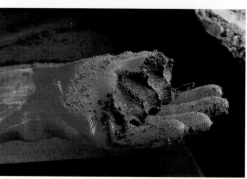

Use fat mud for edges and vertical surfaces. Grijalva's helper, Martin Arellano, builds a layer of fat mud along the edge of the sink cutout. The limed mortar sticks to surfaces and holds its shape.

type-S or comparable lime. These three ingredients are mixed thoroughly before clean water is added. Consistency is crucial. If the mortar is too wet, it won't stay on the trowel. If it's too dry, it won't stick to the wall. We mix a batch of this mortar first, but before applying any of it, we install wooden screed strips on vertical surfaces to determine the depth of the mud bed. Make the strips ½ in. thick and nail them right to the wall over the wire. We use 1½-in. drywall nails, which are easy to pull out later; avoid nailing the screed to a stud. Screed strips should be placed near edges and at intervals so that you will be able to span the distance between them with a straightedge.

We work fat mud firmly into the chicken wire on all vertical surfaces. This is called a scratch coat, and it's essential for getting the rest of the mortar bed to stay put. We bank fat mud against all the cap metal along outside edges, from the top of the metal down to the deck at about a 45° angle. Finally, fat mud is used around all deck penetrations, such as the sink cutout, because it holds its shape there better than deck mud (photo, above right).

After troweling a generous layer of fat mud on the backsplash area, we use a length of straight aluminum or wood to screed the surface, then fill any low spots and screed again. At this point, we remove the screed strips that were nailed to the wall and gently fill in the voids with mortar. Any excess may be cut away once the mortar has firmed up.

Deck mud is used to fill in the remainder of the countertop. It consists of 5 parts sand and 1 part portland cement. Mix these ingredients thoroughly before adding water—and remember to keep the mix dry (top left photos). It should not ooze through your fingers. Trowel and pack down the deck mud over the deck to an elevation slightly higher than the cap metal.

We do not use wooden screeds on the countertop. Instead, we use a level to create several flat spots and then tamp in lengths of cap metal to guide the aluminum straightedge. Locations for these screed pads are somewhat strategic. They need to be placed at all turns in the counter as well as at intermediate locations to allow the straightedge to cover the entire countertop.

With both types of mortar in place, Grijalva uses an aluminum straightedge to screed the countertop. One end rides on a piece of cap metal that has been leveled and tamped in the mortar.

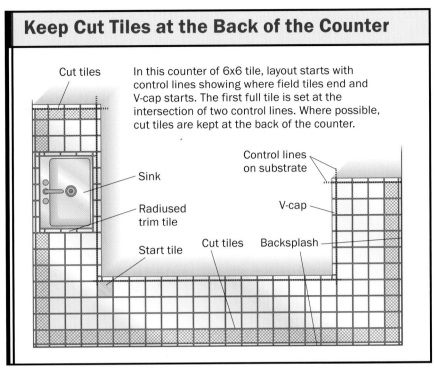

Keep Cut Tiles at the Back of the Counter

Cut tiles

In this counter of 6x6 tile, layout starts with control lines showing where field tiles end and V-cap starts. The first full tile is set at the intersection of two control lines. Where possible, cut tiles are kept at the back of the counter.

Control lines on substrate

Sink

Radiused trim tile

V-cap

Start tile

Cut tiles

Backsplash

The cap metal at the edges of the counter also acts as a screed. Once you have spread enough mortar on the top, use a straight-edge to screed off the excess (photo, above), fill the low spots and screed again, then re-move the cap-metal pieces used as screed pads. A wooden trowel will not bring water to the surface as a metal tool will, although one last pass with a flat-edged metal trowel leaves a smoother finish.

Fundamentals Make Tile Layout Less Complicated

Laying out individual tiles so that the job is aesthetically pleasing as a whole is no easy feat, especially in those kitchens where counters wrap around corners or make an-gled jogs. It is virtually a given that tiles will have to be cut somewhere. The trick is in making the cuts where they are least obvi-ous and making the tile pattern as a whole pleasing to the eye.

A few fundamentals will help. First, try to lay out the counter so that no tile you set is less than half its original size. Second, never break, or interrupt, grout lines unless you are using two different-size tiles or unless you can dramatically improve the layout by doing so. Grout lines generally should be continuous as they move from the counter-top to the backsplash or up other vertical surfaces. Although it's a matter of personal preference, I look at countertop penetrations such as a cooktop or sink as unavoidable in-terruptions in the tile job as a whole—not something the tile layout should be maneu-vered around.

We begin setting tiles immediately after the mortar bed has been leveled and tamped. But first, we mark out reference lines along the edges of the counter to indi-cate where the V-cap starts (photos, p. 102). I start with full tiles on as many of the lead-ing or open edges of the counter as possible (drawing, above). Open edges are those that do not abut a restraining edge, such as a wall or a raised counter. Cut tiles should go at the back. In many of the kitchens we do,

With the mortar bed tamped and leveled, a piece of V-cap is used to set layout lines. Grijalva uses a utility knife to mark the inside edge.

After marking all counter edges with the V-cap, Grijalva and his helper snap chalklines. These control lines are essential for setting straight courses of field tile.

L- and U-shaped counters are common, so we are careful to start the first full tile as shown in the drawing. This layout ensures the greatest number of full-field tiles and the fewest disruptions in the overall pattern.

It would be impossible to cover all the layout problems you may have to wrestle with. For this reason, consider using a story pole, which you can make yourself. Lay tiles in a row on the floor with the desired grout spacing. Place a length of wood alongside these tiles, and mark it where tiles fall. You can place the story pole at any point on the area to be tiled and see right away what your cuts will look like. If you're tiling for someone other than yourself, it may be best to involve him or her in layout decisions, and a story pole can be a big help in explaining the options. You also can simply lay out tiles to test a pattern, but a story pole is faster. You may find that starting the tile in a different spot yields the best overall countertop pattern with the fewest awkward cuts.

Sinks can be handled in several ways. One option is to set a self-rimming sink on top of the field tile once the counter is done. For a neater appearance, set the sink in the mortar bed before field tile is laid, then use trim tiles with a radiused edge as a border.

Set Field Tiles in an Even Layer of Thinset Adhesive

The adhesive used to bond tile to either a mortar bed or a cement board is called dry-set mortar, or thinset. We use basic thinset on ceramic and other pervious tiles. Latex- or polymer-modified thinset is a good choice for impervious tile such as porcelain. Instructions printed on the bag will tell you which size notched trowel to use and tell you how to apply the thinset. It is crucial to follow the instructions exactly. You should mix only enough thinset that can be tiled over within 15 minutes. Don't let it skim over.

The only spot where we don't use thinset is on the edges where V-cap tiles are installed. We have seen these tiles crack when thinset is used, possibly because the thinset makes a rigid bond that's tough on the 90° edge of the V-cap if there's any flex in the rough top. We now use premixed tile

Inside Angles Call for Mitered Edge Pieces

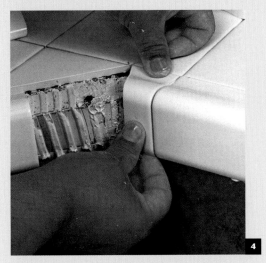

Mitering the two pieces of V-cap meeting in this 45° corner will make the neatest job. To start, Grijalva uses two offcuts to establish the corner, then measures for the first mitered piece of V-cap.

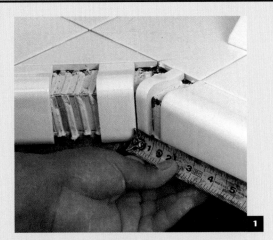

By aligning one pencil mark on the slot in the saw's sliding table and the other mark with the blade, you can make an accurate miter cut on a tile saw.

For all exposed edges that must be cut, a tile saw followed by a pumice stone gives a much smoother finish than a snap cutter. Use a snap cutter where tile edges will be buried.

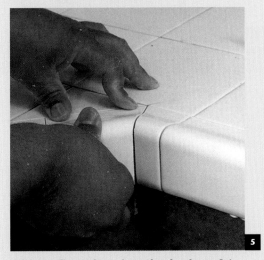

This piece of mitered V-cap fits the space perfectly, but it's safer to dry-fit both pieces before applying any mastic.

With the first mitered section in place, Grijalva can mark and cut the second piece of V-cap. The result is a neat, well-fitting corner.

Special Pieces

Specially shaped tile pieces make fast work of inside and outside corners. Plastic wedges will help, too (photo, below). Sold by tile suppliers, they make it easy to get the top edge of the backsplash to line up perfectly.

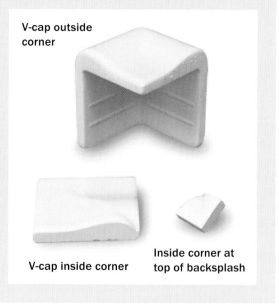

V-cap outside corner

V-cap inside corner

Inside corner at top of backsplash

Radiused Corners Need Special Fitting

Grijalva pencils in the line where a field tile will have to be cut to fit a radiused corner. He cuts the curves on a tile saw by nibbling to the line. Pie-shaped pieces of V-cap, cut by eye and tested until they fit, complete the corner.

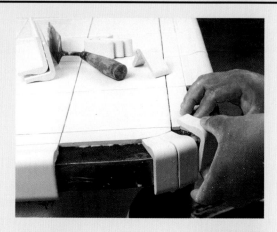

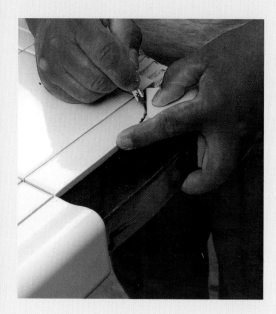

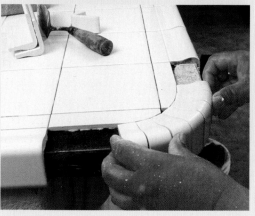

Keep grout lines straight. When turning a corner, a framing square prevents wandering grout lines. If tile is being set over a mortar bed before it is cured, be careful not to mar the surface.

A straightedge makes diagonal cuts easier. Grijalva lays dry tile on the mortar bed, then marks the tile with a straightedge. After the tiles have been cut, thinset and tile are brought to the layout line.

mastic for these edge pieces. Mastic stays more pliable than thinset, and the edge tiles don't crack.

Thinset should not ooze up more than two-thirds of the way into the grout joint. If that seems to be happening, you may be using a trowel with too deep a notch, or you may not be applying a consistent amount of thinset. When you get too much thinset in a joint, simply rake it out.

We start with a full tile at the intersection of control lines on the countertop. Many tiles are produced with spacers, called lugs, on the edges. You can set the tiles together or space them farther apart, but never wider than the thickness of the tile so that the grout won't crack. To help keep the joints consistent if the spacing is greater than the lugs provide, you can use plastic spacers available where you buy tile. But don't count on spacers to keep the lines straight—that is what control lines and straightedges are for. A framing square helps to keep tiles aligned when turning corners (photo, left), and aluminum angle stock is invaluable for staying on track—we keep several different lengths on all our jobs. A good alternative is a straight piece of wood.

Some counter shapes require a number of tiles to be cut on a diagonal at the counter edge (photo, right). In these situations, we lay these tiles out dry (no thinset) so that they can be marked with a pencil and straightedge. Once the tiles are cut on a tile saw, the thinset can be troweled on and the tiles set in place. Inside corners and curved edges can be tricky, but they are easily managed with a little care (photos, p. 103).

A tile saw is indispensable. Rent one if you can't find a friend who will loan you one. A saw produces a clean cut that needs only a little touchup with a pumice stone. Snap cutters are faster, but the edge isn't smooth enough to be shown on the finished counter. We use snap cutters when the edge will be buried, such as at the back of the counter where the backsplash hides any roughness. And when you pick up your tile supplies, make sure you ask for plastic wedges and corner pieces.

Grouting Is the Final Step

Grouting is easy if you follow two simple rules. First, use the proper tools—a smooth, hard-rubber grout float and top-quality hydro sponges. Second, and most important, follow the grout manufacturer's instructions. Even the best tools can't salvage

Cement Board Is a Quick Alternative to a Mortar Bed

In Dennis Hourany's part of the country, the West Coast, a mortar bed is usually specified as the substrate for a tiled kitchen counter. But tilesetters in other regions may prefer a cement-board underlayment, such as Durock or WonderBoard. These panels, made of portland cement and reinforcing fiberglass mesh, speed up preparation of the tile substrate considerably.

For Tom Meehan, a tilesetter in Harwich, Massachusetts, cement board is the substrate of choice for kitchen counters (drawing, facing page). It bonds well with the thinset adhesive used to set the tile, and it can be installed quickly.

Cement board is fairly easy to cut (left photos, facing page). Treat the material like drywall—score a line with a utility knife a few times, snap the board along the line and then cut the back of the board along the break. You can get a smoother cut with a circular saw and carbide blade, but be careful. Breathing the dust is unhealthy. Meehan suggests cutting the board outside and making sure you wear a respirator.

Before installing the cement board, Meehan screws down a layer of ¾-in., exterior-grade plywood on the top of the cabinet. Screw heads should be flush with the surface. Next is a layer of thinset mortar or construction adhesive (top center photo, facing page), followed by ½-in. thick cement board. If you're using construction adhesive, work quickly because it begins to skim over in about five minutes and loses its pliability. Meehan presses the cement board into place and jiggles it gently to even out the adhesive

beneath it. The cement board is attached with 1¼-in. galvanized drywall screws 8 in. o.c. (top right photo, facing page). You may want to drill pilot holes.

If kitchen cabinets already have laminate counters that are structurally sound, you can leave them in place and put down ¼-in. or ⁵⁄₁₆-in. cement board right on top of the laminate. Laminate should be scuffed with a 50-grit sandpaper first. The total substrate should be no less than 1¼ in. thick.

Edges can be handled a couple of ways. In the installation featured here, Meehan brings the cement board flush to the edge of the plywood and then finishes the edge with a layer of thinset and fiberglass mesh tape (bottom right photo, facing page). Another approach is to finish the outside edge with a vertical strip of cement board, and then apply a layer of thinset and mesh tape.

Cement board is available in thicknesses of ¼ in., ⁵⁄₁₆ in., ⁷⁄₁₆ in., ½ in., and ⅝ in. Sheets may be 32 in., 36 in., or 48 in. wide.

Although Meehan thinks cement board is best, another possibility is a material called Dens-Shield. Georgia-Pacific says Dens-Shield is one-third lighter than portland-cement backer board and is more water resistant than cement-board products. The company says the board has a proprietary heat-cured surface with a silicone-treated core embedded with glass mats.

Scott Gibson is a freelance writer and a contributing editor for Fine Homebuilding.

1. Score cement board with a knife. Tilesetter Tom Meehan uses a utility knife and a straight-edge to score a piece of Durock cement board.

2. Score the back, too. After snapping the cement board along the score line, Meehan cuts through the back of the sheet, like working with wallboard.

3. The board should break cleanly. Once fibers on the back of the board have been severed, the sheet should break cleanly along the score line.

Cement Board Makes a Good Bond with Thinset Adhesive

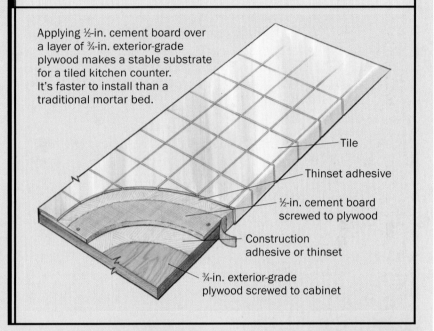

Applying ½-in. cement board over a layer of ¾-in. exterior-grade plywood makes a stable substrate for a tiled kitchen counter. It's faster to install than a traditional mortar bed.

Tile

Thinset adhesive

½-in. cement board screwed to plywood

Construction adhesive or thinset

¾-in. exterior-grade plywood screwed to cabinet

4. Bond the cement board to the counter. A bead of construction adhesive may be used to bond the cement board to the rough top.

5. Screws hold the cement board down. Galvanized drywall screws 8 in. o.c. keep the cement board in place while the adhesive sets up.

6. Finish edges with thinset. Fiberglass mesh tape and a thin layer of thinset adhesive finish the edges. This substrate is now ready for tile.

Sources

Custom Building Products®
13001 Seal Beach Blvd.
Seal Beach, CA 90740
(800) 272-8786
www.custombuilding
products.com
WonderBoard

**Georgia-Pacific®
Corp.**
133 Peachtree St., N.E.
Atlanta, GA 30303
(404) 652-4000
www.gp.com
Dens-Shield

**United States
Gypsum (USG)**
125 South Franklin
Chicago, IL 60606
(800) 874-4968
www.usg.com
Durock

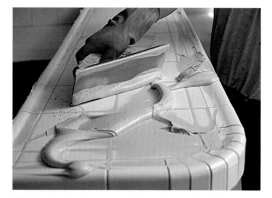

Wait a day before grouting. Once the thinset has cured, mix grout to a creamy consistency and force the material into the gaps between tiles with a hard rubber float. Work the float at an angle.

A tile sponge cleans up the residue. Be careful not to dig out any grout, and rinse the sponge frequently.

Arellano uses a generous pad of clean cheese-cloth to remove the haze left by the tile sponge. The surface polishes quickly.

a job when the grout has been mixed or applied improperly. Tile adhesive should cure for at least 24 hours before grout is applied. Before getting started, remove any loose material from the joints. You also may want to apply a grout release to the surface of unglazed tiles to prevent staining.

Grout stays workable for about two hours. You should restir the grout mix periodically as you work, but do not add any more liquid to it. If the grout becomes too stiff to work, throw it out and make a fresh batch.

Once the grout is mixed and you've removed any debris from the joints, use the hard-rubber float to force grout into the joints (top left photo). Work diagonally using enough pressure to ensure the joints are filled. Then remove excess grout with the edge of the float. After allowing the grout to set up for 15 minutes or so, wet and ring out a sponge and wipe the tile diagonally (bottom left photo). For your final pass, use each side of the sponge only once before wringing it out. You can use a soft, dry cloth to polish off the haze that forms after about 40 minutes (photo, right). Misting the grout with water several times a day for two or three days will increase its strength and prevent cracking. But wait 10 days before applying any grout sealer—an important step that increases water and stain resistance.

Dennis Hourany has been a licensed tile contractor for 22 years. He owns Elite Tile in Walnut Creek, California.

Tiling over a Laminate Counter

■ BY DAVID HART

I tear out tons of tub surrounds and sheet vinyl every year and install ceramic tile. That type of remodeling makes up the bulk of my work. Other than an occasional mud-set floor, I use cementitious backer board as tile underlayment on walls and floors. After having mixed results with plywood, I found that backer board also works great for countertop renovations.

The major advantage to installing backerboard over an existing laminate countertop is that it keeps down the total cost of the tile installation. Instead of building a new countertop, I set the tile on a sheet of ¼-in. backer board that's screwed to the old laminate. The backer board provides a sturdy, stable substrate for the tile, it saves me a day (or more) of labor, and it can knock several hundred dollars off the total cost of the project. (Obviously, this method won't work on postformed counters.)

Why not install the tile directly on the countertop? It doesn't work. I learned the hard way that latex- or polymer-modified thinsets don't bond well to plastic laminate, even though a mortar manufacturer assured me that they would. After two installation failures involving only thinset, I now over-

Although backer board can be scored with a utility knife and snapped, an angle grinder fitted with a diamond blade cuts a cleaner line faster.

lay the laminate with backer board and haven't had a callback since.

Make Sure the Original Counter Is Sound

Because a new sink is often part of a counter renovation, my first step is to determine the size of the new sink cutout. If the new sink is smaller than the original, I have to rebuild the counter to give the sink proper support before overlaying the top with backer board. If the new sink dimensions are larger, I cut the countertop to the correct size and continue with the installation. (It's also worth noting here that unless they have flexible water supplies, most sinks need to be re-plumbed due to the increased depth of the counter.)

I also check the condition of the counter's particleboard. Prolonged exposure to steam from a dishwasher or water seepage from around the sink can turn particleboard into little more than loose sawdust. The best way to check is to crawl into the base cabinet and examine the underside of the countertop

Narrower edge strips are more easily concealed. To ensure that the tile covers the backer board, the author keeps the edge strips at least ¼ in. back from the counter's edge.

with a flashlight. If I can dig particleboard apart with a screwdriver or pocketknife, or if it's swelling from exposure to moisture, then the damage is probably too severe to use this installation method. Scrap the existing top, rebuild it, and quit reading this article.

All laminate countertops will move when you pound a fist on them, but excessive movement will lead to cracked grout joints and, eventually, loose tiles. Cement backer boards help to tighten any floor or counter-top if installed properly, but bouncy or spongy tops need to be fixed or scrapped. Often, a few screws driven up into the countertop through the cabinets' corner brackets will stiffen a bouncy top.

It's also important at this early stage to measure the height of the tiles that cover the edge of the counter (called V-cap) and compare that dimension to the height of the countertop's finished edge. The V-cap should cover the countertop edge and backer board. Typical V-cap covers about 1¾ in., which doesn't leave much tile hanging below the substrate; some run deeper, and others run a little shallower. I also make sure the cabinet drawers don't hit the tile overhang.

Cutting Cement Backer Board

If I need to keep the job site clean, sometimes I cut backer board with a utility knife and a straightedge. Although it's slightly more expensive than other backer board, Durock is somewhat softer and easier to cut with a standard utility knife. Yes, I burn through blades, but it's quick and virtually dust-free.

Utility knives don't work well on harder, slicker boards such as Wonderboard, so to cut those types of board, I rely on a right-angle grinder with 4-in. dry-cut diamond blade (photo, p. 109). A vital piece of equipment for compound or circular cuts as well, this tool throws a cloud of dust anytime I cut cement board with it, so I never use it in an enclosed space.

I always lay the board in place dry to check the fit; I usually allow up to a ½-in. gap between the counter and wall and up to a ¼-in. gap between individual pieces of board. The important thing here is that I don't want the backer board to extend beyond the edges of the top. After I cut the backer board to fit the existing top, I cut strips for the counter's edge about ¼ in. narrower than the edge of the countertop (photo, facing page) so that the backer board doesn't stick out below the bottom of the edge cap.

Modified Thinset and Screws Make a Better Bond

By itself, ¼-in. backer board offers no additional strength when attached directly to the substrate; a layer of the thinset beneath the backer board fills the voids and creates a vacuum that is nearly impossible to break. I never skip this step. Unmodified mortar doesn't provide any bond to the laminate, although it will stick to the backer board, so I always spend the few extra dollars and get latex or polymer-modified thinset, which cures harder than unmodified mortar and allows a small amount of deflection.

It's important to mix thinset with the proper amount of water. As a rule, too much water will create a weak bond; too little makes the product tough to trowel, and it may not bond to the tile or backer board properly. I try to mix it so that it has a smooth, creamy consistency. If the mix clings to my trowel without running off and still spreads easily, then I know I've got a good mix.

After mixing a batch of thinset, I trowel it onto the counter (photo, left) with a ¼-in. notch trowel, trying not to spread more thinset than I can use in 10 or 15 minutes.

> *A layer of the thinset beneath the backer board fills the voids and creates a vacuum that is nearly impossible to break.*

Like peanut butter spread between two pieces of bread, thinset troweled onto the counter will fill voids beneath the backer board and strengthen the substrate.

Faced with a day of driving screws into substrate, the author uses an autofeed screw gun that starts and seats each screw much faster than by hand.

For an experienced tilesetter, that can mean the entire counter, but for those new to this type of work, that might mean covering a small section at one time. Once a section of counter is covered, I lay the backer board in place and screw it down.

Because the board is only ¼ in. thick, I use screws that are 1 in. long. Longer screws might protrude through the bottom of the particleboard and give someone a nasty scrape. I like to space the screws about 6 in. apart on the perimeter of the board and 8 in. to 10 in. apart on the inside. Although I have used loose screws and a screw gun, I usually rely on a Makita® autofeed screw gun (right photo, p. 111); it's just quicker. I try to make sure that there are no bubbles in the backer board and that I seat the screw heads flush or slightly below the surface.

Tile Layout: Big Tiles Are Better

Once the counter is ready, I take time for a careful tile layout. Nothing will ruin an installation more than a poor layout. For this project, I first installed the 6-in. V-caps, starting from the outside corners and working toward the wall (photo, left). I butter the backside of each tile as I go, which makes the next step cleaner. Once the edge is complete, I lay out the interior tile pattern dry (photo, right) to see which tiles will have to be cut. On a perfect installation, I would end up with full tiles across the full width of the counter, but that never happens. The best installation will have the largest tiles possible in the most visible areas. And I'll often try to cut a small amount from tiles on

These narrow right-angle tiles form a border for the square field tiles. Starting at the exterior bullnose corners, the V-caps are laid out first in an equal pattern that ends at a wall or a mitered inside corner.

To ensure a well-spaced layout, the author places whole tiles across the space, using a center mark as a reference. The remaining space is divided into two partial tiles.

Grout works best when spread in small areas. Worked into tile joints with a rubber float, grout tends to set up quickly, and it becomes difficult to remove from the tile surface. A clean, damp sponge is the best tool to wipe excess grout from tiles and to smooth grout lines.

both sides of the layout rather than cutting a large amount from the tiles on one side.

Once I've checked the layout, I start applying enough thinset to keep me going for about 10 minutes. If the mix sits on the backer board for much longer than that, it starts to skim over, and then it won't bond with the tile.

Apply Small Areas of Grout

After the tile is set, I wait a day for the thinset to cure before I start grouting. Most grout has a modifier in it, which creates a stronger, more stain-resistant grout, so there's no need to add latex to the dry pow-

der. The grout/water mix should be stiffer than toothpaste, but loose enough to push across the tile without great force.

Using a rubber float, I usually won't spread more grout than I can work in about 10 minutes. I don't allow the grout to sit on the tile surface for long, either; once it has hardened, the grout is difficult to remove. I use a large damp sponge to smooth the joints and to wipe off the face of the tile. It's important not to wipe too much out of the joints, to rinse the sponge frequently, and to wring the excess water out of the sponge. Too much water can discolor or weaken grout.

David Hart is a tile contractor and outdoors writer living in Centreville, Virginia.

Sources

Custom Building Products
13001 Seal Beach Blvd.
Seal Beach, CA 90740
(800) 272-8786
www.custombuilding products.com

Makita
14930 Northam St.
La Mirada, CA 90638
(800) 462-5482
www.makita.com

United States Gypsum (USG)
125 South Franklin
Chicago, IL 60606
(800) 874-4968
www.usg.com

An Inside Look at Kitchen Cabinets

■ BY SCOTT GIBSON

At the giant KraftMaid® cabinet factory just outside Cleveland, workers stand by with glue guns and pneumatic nailers as parts for a complete set of kitchen cabinets approach on a conveyor. Drawers, face frames, prefinished panels, shelves, and moldings arrive from all corners of the million-sq.-ft.-plant. Although the customer who ordered this kitchen may have taken months to plan its every detail, KraftMaid assemblers will put it together in 15 minutes. Cabinets are shipped about a week after the order has arrived.

Did you think your new kitchen cabinets would be hand-built by fussy artisans? Guess again. Cabinets are a $6 billion industry, and they pour off assembly lines like hubcaps or lawn chairs. If that prospect unsettles you, consider a smaller company, one like Rutt® Custom Cabinetry of Goodville, Pennsylvania. Here, door panels are matched for color and figure, one board at a time. A specialist is standing by to custom-blend a paint color. The catch? Rutt charges more than twice as much, and you can count on waiting 40 or 50 days to get your order.

KraftMaid and Rutt are only two among hundreds of cabinet manufacturers. Yet they help to illustrate the many choices buyers will face before plunking down thousands of dollars for a new kitchen.

Manufactured Kitchens Fall into Three General Categories

To help make sense of what's available, the industry has traditionally divided cabinets into three grades: stock, semicustom, and custom. The labels don't mean as much as they once did, but they are still a good starting point.

Stock cabinets are at the low end of the market. Available in limited styles and finishes and with fewer options, stock cabinets are built in standard sizes in increments of 3 in. in width. They are manufactured and then stockpiled, without regard to who will buy them. Semicustom cabinets are built to order, also on a 3-in. grid, and offer more choices when it comes to styles, accessories, and finishes. Materials may be of higher quality. Custom cabinets, such as those from Rutt, are built to fit the available floor space exactly with just about any option the customer is willing to pay for. They are the most expensive of all.

And then there are the small shops, the local cabinetmakers found in virtually every corner of the country. Working on one job at a time, these shops turn out cabinets designed for just one client. Detailing, construction, and wood selection may range from ordinary to exquisite. Yet these cabinets are not manufactured in the same sense as factory-built, mass-produced goods.

Any cabinet is a sum of its parts, and the choices can seem overwhelmingly complicated. Assessing quality is not always easy. Many manufacturers submit their cabinets to the Kitchen Cabinet Manufacturers Association[SM] for voluntary testing and certification. Although the process is wide-ranging and rigorous (roughly half of those seeking certification for the first time will flunk), it's not useful for comparing individual components such as drawers, doors, and cabinet boxes. And makers of high-end cabinetry may skip the test altogether.

Whatever the cabinet industry's tests show, it pays to buy cabinets that are carefully built from good-quality materials and hardware. To me, that means avoiding cabinets made from paper-coated panels or ones with thin shelves that bend under pressure. Drawers should open smoothly, without wobbling. A finish should be silky to the touch, without any visible sanding marks. In short, buyers should seek cabinets that look and feel as if they are solidly made.

Prices vary as widely as quality. Bottom-of-the-line stock cabinets for a kitchen of roughly 120 sq. ft. are available for less than $2,500, not including countertops and installation. According to estimates provided by both KraftMaid and Merillat[SM], one of the country's largest cabinet manufacturers, a better-quality kitchen might range from just over $5,000 to $12,800, depending on materials and accessories. A custom-manufactured kitchen can approach $20,000.

The following pages look in detail at four manufactured base cabinets that are typical of what's on the market. More expensive often means more quality and a longer life. But getting the best value also should include a careful look at the many differences in construction, hardware, finish, and materials.

*Prices from 1999.

Scott Gibson *is a freelance writer and is a contributing editor for* Fine Homebuilding.

Cabinet Boxes: Your Kitchen's Foundation

A salesman may call the cabinet French provincial, Shaker, or Arts and Crafts, but from a construction standpoint, manufactured cabinets are one of two types: traditional face frame or frameless. In a face-frame cabinet, a rigid frame made of ¾-in. solid wood is attached to the front of a plywood or particleboard box. Face frames create square door and drawer openings while adding strength to the cabinet and helping to keep it square during construction, shipping, and installation. Depending on the type of hinge used, some or all of the frame is visible when doors and drawers are installed. In a frameless cabinet, overlay doors and drawer fronts hide the cabinet box. Often made from melamine, which is particleboard covered by a thin layer of plastic laminate, these cabinet boxes are usually held together with dowels and glue.

The days of solid-wood construction are long gone, mainly because panel products such as plywood, particleboard, or medium-density fiberboard make a stronger, more stable cabinet at a lower cost. Upper and lower cabinet boxes are now typically constructed of particleboard topped with wood veneer, vinyl paper,

(continued)

$115

Frameless Melamine Is Inexpensive, Easy to Clean

Frameless cabinets, such as this melamine base unit from LesCare Kitchens of Waterbury, Connecticut, use a full overlay door and drawer front that span the width of the carcase. Upgrading the door and drawer front to a more durable high-pressure laminate raises the price of this cabinet to $180.

1, 2 Carcase: Cabinet sides are ¾-in. melamine-faced particleboard with a ¼-in. back and a ¾-in. floor. Parts are assembled with glued dowel joints and are reinforced with full-width stretchers.

3 Shelf: Held in place by adjustable plastic clips, the ¾-in. melamine shelf is 12 in. deep, about half the depth of the cabinet itself.

4 Drawer: Sides of ⅝-in. melamine are doweled and glued together with a ¼-in. bottom and a thermofoil drawer front (medium-density fiberboard wrapped in plastic).

5 Door: A full-overlay thermofoil door is hung on adjustable hinges that can be removed without any tools, making it easy to pop off the door for a thorough cleaning.

melamine, or the same kind of high-pressure laminate used on countertops. Boxes of veneer-core plywood, lighter and stronger than particleboard, also are available, but often cost more. Whether plywood or particleboard, more expensive cabinets tend to use thicker material for cabinet boxes and shelves.

A solvent-based varnish is a common choice for kitchen cabinets. It's tough and durable. In cheaper cabinets, the top coat may look glossy and rough, with some sanding marks still visible. Many companies, however, offer sophisticated, layered finishes in many colors or wood tones.

$125

Stock Face-Frame Cabinet Made with Lighter Materials

This cabinet, made by Kitchen Kompact of Jeffersonville, Indiana, uses a traditional face frame to reinforce the front of the carcase. In this price range, some materials are likely to be relatively thin with a simulated wood-grain finish.

6 Carcase: Materials include sides of ½-in. wood-veneer particleboard, and a back of ⅛-in. vinyl-covered hardboard. The cabinet floor is ¼-in. vinyl-covered hardboard that flexes under a load. Corner blocks that reinforce the cabinet are stapled in place, but not all of the staples hit their target.

7 Shelf: Not adjustable and only ½ in. thick, the 11-in.-wide shelf is made of vinyl-covered particleboard.

8 Drawer: Sides are ⅜-in. fiberboard faced in a wood-grain vinyl with a solid drawer front of red oak.

9 Door: A wood-veneer panel is set in a frame of solid oak. Hinges cannot be adjusted.

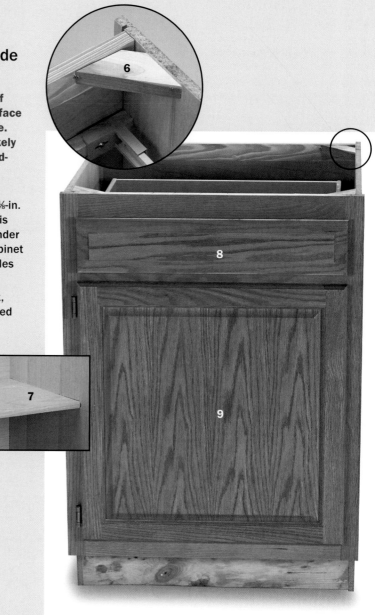

$300

For More Money, a Sturdier Cabinet

This semicustom KraftMaid cabinet has several advantages over lower-priced alternatives, including heavier materials and more durable construction.

10, 11 Carcase: This cabinet box is made from ½-in. veneer-core plywood with a ⅜-in. plywood back and a fully finished interior. Two ⁷⁄₁₆-in. plywood stretchers reinforce the top of the cabinet.

12 Shelf: A ¾-in. plywood shelf runs the full depth of the cabinet. Held in place by plastic clips, the shelf is fully adjustable.

13 Drawer: A dovetailed hardwood drawer box is made with ¾-in. sides with a ¼-in. bottom and a ¾-in. hardwood drawer front.

14 Door: The solid door frame of ¾-in. maple has a solid-wood panel on adjustable hinges.

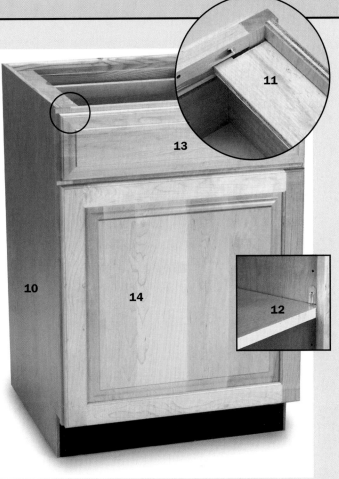

$700

Top of the Line, with a Price Tag to Match

This Rutt Custom Cabinetry base unit has a sophisticated painted finish and an inset door, making it look more like traditional furniture-grade cabinetry. Good quality hardware operates smoothly.

15, 16 Carcase: The cabinet box is made from ⅝-in. veneer-core plywood with a ¼-in. veneered back of medium-density fiberboard. A full dust panel reinforces the top of the cabinet.

17 Shelf: Although the retaining clip on the shelf is plastic, the weight is actually carried by a concealed metal pin, which is stronger. Adjustable and 18 in. deep, the shelf is made from ¾-in. veneer-core plywood.

18 Drawer: The drawer is made from ⅝-in. hardwood joined with glue and dowels at the corners with top-quality undermount drawer slides. The drawer has a ¼-in. bottom.

19 Door: A traditionally mortised and tenoned door frame has a beaded detail on the inside edge and is hung with decorative butt hinges, which are not adjustable.

Drawers: A Sturdy Box Can Take a Lot of Abuse

Few kitchen components get as much wear and tear as a drawer. Before the introduction of modern drawer slides, a wood drawer box ran on wooden runners fastened to the inside of the cabinet. Often overloaded and yanked on unmercifully in sticky summer weather, drawers had a hard life. Good drawer slides incorporating plastic or metal rollers have eliminated much of that stress, making drawer construction less of an issue than it used to be. Even so, a drawer made of undersize material and running on cheap slides will be a never-ending source of irritation.

Solid hardwood traditionally has been the material of choice for good-quality drawer boxes. One big advantage is that the material does not dictate the joint that will be used to join the corners of the box. Solid wood can be dovetailed, doweled, biscuited, or dadoed, and a raw edge will never show. Many drawers also are made from engineered wood: veneered plywood, particleboard, melamine, or medium-density fiberboard. These drawers, common in frameless cabinetry, are often glued and doweled together. Raw edges must be banded. Plywood or melamine drawers certainly can be durable, but the material should be at least ½ in. thick. Avoid drawers made from thin, vinyl-covered particleboard and nailed at the corners. They feel flimsy, and they are more likely to come apart over time.

A standard drawer slide is an epoxy-coated, three-quarter extension unit rated at 75 lb. But full-extension slides, rated to 100 lb. and allowing access to even the back of the drawer, may be available as an upgrade. Undermount slides stay out of sight and, like other hardware, come in various levels of quality. The best are made from heavy-duty materials and quiet, smoothly operating rollers or ball bearings, such as the Tandem slide by Blum, used on Rutt cabinets.

Doweled hardwood drawer box. Light and strong, this ⅝-in. box of yellow poplar is joined with dowels at the corners and comes with a ½-in. plywood drawer bottom. That may be overkill in a narrow drawer, but a bottom this thick won't sag. Self-closing Blum undermount drawer slides are hidden, and they perform flawlessly.

Dovetailed hardwood. Always the darling of the cabinet trade, a dovetail drawer should last a long time. This one has sides of ¾-in. hardwood and a ³⁄₁₆-in. plywood bottom (a heavier drawer bottom would be better in a wider drawer intended for heavy objects). Undermount slides are out of the way, but they do not operate as smoothly or seem as sturdy as those made by Blum.

Marginal materials and construction. Drawers such as these are unlikely to give you a lifetime of dependable service. Faced with a drawer front of red oak, the drawer box is ⅜-in. medium-density fiberboard faced in wood-grain vinyl and joined with nails and glue. The ³⁄₁₆-in. drawer bottom flexes under pressure.

Doweled melamine. Typical for a frameless cabinet, this drawer box is made of ⅝-in. melamine, doweled at the corners, with a ¼-in. bottom. The three-quarter extension epoxy-coated slide (this one by Blum) operates smoothly. The gap between the applied drawer front and the front of this box shouldn't be there.

Drawers made from wood parts are by far the most common, but metal drawers also are available. One variety found in some frameless cabinetry has epoxy-coated metal sides attached to a standard melamine drawer front. The drawer side incorporates part of the slide mechanism.

Where to Buy a Kitchen

Manufacturers sell their cabinets through a retail network that includes building-supply stores, lumberyards, and stores specializing in kitchen and bathroom cabinetry. Larger cabinet retailers offer more variety, and those located near big home-improvement centers such as Home Depot[SM] may offer everyone the prices that once were reserved for builders. If you have a particular cabinet brand in mind, the company can provide the name of a nearby retailer.

Driving from store to store is a time-honored way to shop, but doing some homework on the Internet first can help. Many manufacturers maintain their own Web sites where you can browse product offerings, learn more about how their cabinets are built and find out where to buy them. One place to start is with a search engine, where a search for "kitchen cabinets" will turn up companies all over the country. Content can range from specific information on construction techniques and materials to collections of glossy photos. Some cabinet-manufacturing companies offer interactive sites that will help you to design a kitchen layout and to choose various accessories.

For lists of manufacturers, try www.buildingonline.com or www.kitchen-bath.com. Lists are organized so that you can search for a smaller company in your region. Another good resource is www.nkba.org, the home page of the National Kitchen & Bath Association[SM], an industry trade group. You'll find design tips, budgeting information and industry links for cabinets and other products. The Kitchen Cabinet Manufacturers Association's site (www.kcma.org) details the association's certification process for kitchen cabinets, valuable information for anyone in the market for a new kitchen.

Cabinet Doors Are a Visual Focal Point

Manufacturers devote a lot of attention to the doors on their cabinets for good reason: Along with drawer fronts, these parts are dominant visual elements in any kitchen. A single company may offer dozens of door styles. Many cabinet manufacturers do not build their own doors, buying them instead from vendors such as Conestoga® Wood Specialties Inc. in East Earl, Pennsylvania, which makes some 5.5 million doors a year.

On frame-and-panel doors, virtually everyone now uses what's called a cope-and-stick joint in which the interlocking edges of the frame parts form the glue joint. Although this joint might horrify traditionalists, it is by now time-tested and strong enough. Be wary of any door showing gaps in the joinery. Raised door panels may be either solid wood with a profile milled into the outside edge (left photo) or engineered

wood faced in a thin wood veneer (center photo). Profiles will be crisper, and panels more durable, when of solid wood. Thermofoil doors (right photo) mimic frame-and-panel styles but are made of engineered wood covered in plastic.

Some doors have mitered corners, like a picture frame, which are doweled or splined together. Seasonal wood movement makes this type of joint more likely to open up than other designs, just like mitered door and window casings.

Most kitchen cabinets have overlay doors, meaning the doors overlap the door opening. A full overlay door, such as the one on the melamine cabinet on p. 117, covers the front of the cabinet completely. Because the doors are slightly bigger than their openings, overlay doors don't require any fitting. Less common are inset doors, which are housed in the door opening.

A step up in a wood design. This maple KraftMaid door has a solid-wood raised panel and a smoother, less brassy finish than the door on a budget cabinet. The cope-and-stick joinery is essentially the same. The color and figure of the maple pieces used in both the panel and the frame are not perfectly matched.

A stock frame-and-panel door. A solid red-oak frame surrounds a veneered panel. Frame pieces are joined at the corners in a cope-and-stick pattern, a standard door joint. The panel is a very thin wood veneer over particleboard, not solid wood. Some sanding marks are evident on the inside of the door.

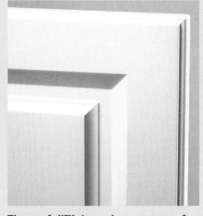

Thermofoil™ doors have a core of engineered wood. A traditional frame-and-panel look-alike, this door is actually a vinyl-like plastic formed around a core of medium-density fiberboard milled by a computer-controlled router. Unlike other kinds of laminated doors, this one has only a single seam. MDF is heavy and stable.

When closed, inset doors are flush with the face of the cabinet, making the cabinet look more like a piece of furniture.

Overlay doors are usually hung with cup hinges, which are hidden when the door is closed. Cup hinges allow the door to be adjusted in several directions, making alignment easy for manufacturer and buyer alike. Better hinges have more adjusting points, and some allow the door to be popped off the cabinet without using tools (top left photo).

Door hinges can be a trouble spot for cabinets. According to the Kitchen Cabinet Manufacturers Association, failing hinges are one of the most common reasons that cabinets flunk certification tests. So it pays to check them carefully when looking for cabinets. Avoid hinges that have too much play or feel flimsy.

Easy on and off. This cup hinge allows a door to be popped off without tools.

No adjustments. This economy hinge offers no door adjustments, and it flexes under a load.

Old-style detailing in a painted door. This pine door uses more traditional joinery. Its sand-through finish relies on layers of color and paint, plus sanding, to mimic the effects of years of hard use.

Adjustable cup hinge. This style of cup hinge allows the door to be adjusted in two directions.

Traditional butt hinge. A furniturelike hinge on this door is set into a mortise in the frame.

Choosing Kitchen Countertops

■ BY SCOTT GIBSON

Yearning for the good old days? Take a close look at an old kitchen. Even well-appointed houses were likely to have kitchens that look utilitarian, even stark, when compared with what contemporary cooks expect. Counter space often was provided by a built-in cabinet or dresser with a

Chop where you like. Maple butcher block exudes a visual warmth many other materials lack. Standard thickness is 1½ in., although 4-in.-thick end-grain block is available.

wood top, or even just a big table. Not these days. We want countertops that delight the eye, stand up to heat, keep out food stains, are easy to clean, and are more durable than the deck of a battleship.

Amazingly, a variety of materials, both natural and man-made, manages to fit the bill: plastic resins, sheet metal, wood, stone, ceramic tile, concrete, even slabs of quarried French lava. Prices range from less than $5 per sq. ft. for plastic-laminate countertops to $300 per sq. ft. for granite as rare as blue Brazilian bahai.

In addition to their many practical contributions, countertops also make a big visual and tactile impact. The huge variety of materials—each with its own range of characteristics and cost—allows a kitchen countertop to fit neatly into just about any lifestyle and architectural tradition. Spending thousands of dollars isn't hard to do, but far more economical alternatives also exist. The only trick is wading through all the options. *Prices from 2001.*

Scott Gibson is a freelance writer and contributing editor for Fine Homebuilding. Cost estimates are gathered from manufacturers, retailers, and installers as well as Repair & Remodeling Cost Data by RSMeans. Prices vary by region.

Butcher Block

Built-in Cutting Boards

Butcher block is one of the few totally natural kitchen-countertop materials. Typically made from strips of hard maple, 1½-in.-thick butcher-block counters are glued up to expose wear-resistant edge grain. They can be ordered in sizes up to 12 ft. long and 4 ft. wide for about $30 to $35 per sq. ft. Butcher block can be ordered through local lumberyards and home centers as well as a few large manufacturers. One of them, John Boos & Company, also makes end-grain tops 4 in. thick in sizes up to 60 in. by 38 in. for about $85 per sq. ft.

Among its advantages as a countertop material: It's easy to work and install, has a visual warmth and pleasing resilience, and can be used as a cutting board. Scratches, scorch marks, and other signs of wear and tear can be counted as character, or scraped and sanded away. One drawback is that wood is susceptible to water damage, so butcher block used around the sink should be carefully sealed.

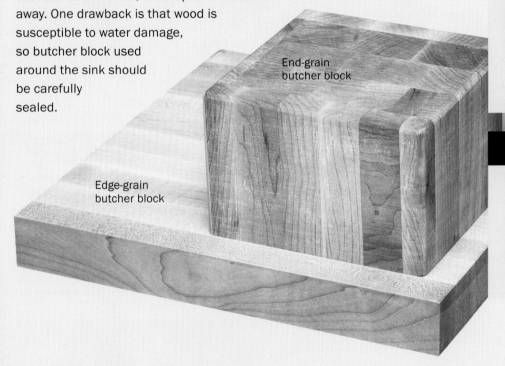

End-grain butcher block

Edge-grain butcher block

Pros/Cons

Pros: Resilient, easy to work, relatively durable, can be used as cutting board, surface can be repaired.
Cons: Will scorch, not as easy to keep clean as some other materials, can stain if unsealed, susceptible to moisture damage around sinks.
Cost: $30 to $85 per sq. ft. uninstalled (shipping, if applicable, extra).

Sources

John Boos & Co.
(217) 347-7701
www.johnboos.com

The Hartwood Lumber Co.
(800) 798-1269
www.hardwood-lumber.com

Concrete

High Style, Potentially High Maintenance

From a design perspective, few countertop materials are as malleable as concrete. Cast upside down in molds or formed in place, concrete counters can be made in virtually any shape and thickness. Made correctly, they are hard, durable, and heat- and scratch-resistant. But cast without proper reinforcement and the correct mix of materials, concrete counters have been known to develop severe cracks as they cure. Even the best of them will stain if not assiduously maintained.

"Sidewalk contractors who do kitchen countertops may be part of the PR problem," says Jeffrey Girard of FormWorks in Raleigh, North Carolina. Counter fabricators such as Girard often cast standard countertops 1½ in. to 2 in. thick, using structural steel and polypropylene fibers to minimize cracking.

Fabricators exert considerable control over the look of the finished product. Girard, for instance, adds pieces of glass and metal to the mix, then grinds the surface to create beautiful, multicolored patterns (top sample, center photo). The work of concrete pioneers like Fu Tung Cheng (photo, above) and Buddy Rhodes (center and bottom sample, center photo) further reveal concrete's versatility.

Concrete's Achilles' heel as a countertop is that it stains easily. "The bottom line is that your concrete counter is going to end up staining no matter what you do," says Eric Olsen, a Berkeley, California, writer who collaborated with Cheng on a book on the topic. "That's part of its charm."

Site-cast counters are another alternative. Oregon builder Thomas Hughes cast this counter upside down in his client's garage from garden-variety portland cement and aggregates.

Samples from Cheng Design

Glass and steel fragments decorate this sample from FormWorks.

Marbleized patterns are typical in the work of Buddy Rhodes.

Pros/Cons

Pros: Versatile, heat resistant, durable, colors and textures easily customized.

Cons: Can stain.

Cost: $60 to $75 per sq. ft. for prefabricated countertops (shipping and installation extra).

Sources

Cheng Design
(510) 849-3272
www.chengdesign.com

FormWorks
(919) 434-5339
www.formworks-nc.com

Buddy Rhodes Studio Inc.
(877) 706-5303
www.buddyrhodes.com

Tile

Design Flexibility, Durability, Low Cost

As a countertop material, ceramic tile offers nearly as much design flexibility as concrete. Tile is available in a huge variety of colors, patterns, textures, sizes, and prices, from mass-produced 4-in. sq. field tile to hand-painted works of art. Installed prices start at about $15 per sq. ft. for a basic counter and go up from there. Loose field tile starts at less than $2 per sq. ft.

Glazed ceramic and porcelain tiles have a glasslike outer layer that makes them long-wearing, highly heat resistant, and nonabsorbent. Tile can be set on a mortar bed or over cement backerboard with thinset mortar. Because it is easy to cut, tile can be formed into counters of just about any shape and size. Damaged tiles can be chiseled out of a counter and replaced.

The downside? For one, tile is really hard. Fragile wine glasses and thin china won't fare well in careless households. You'll need cutting boards on tile surfaces, and because tile counters are made of many pieces, the surface is unlikely to be perfectly flat. Tile's major shortcoming is the grout between the tile. Left untreated, cement-based grout stains easily, and it can be hard to keep clean.

Epoxy grout is one solution. It's good at resisting stains. But epoxy grout yellows with time, especially when exposed to sunlight. Cement-based grout can be sealed to provide some protection. The National Tile Contractors Association says a water-based acrylic sealer, such as Aqua Mix®, is less likely than solvent-based sealers to be eroded by household degreasers and cleaners. The bottom line: The smaller the grout joint, the less maintenance you have.

Pros/Cons

Pros: Versatile, inexpensive, heat resistant, durable, high stain resistance.
Cons: Grout may stain, surface not perfectly flat.
Cost: Materials, including substrate, adhesive, and border tile, from $7 and up per sq. ft. Installation adds $8 to $10 per sq. ft.

Sources

National Tile Contractors Association
(601) 939-2071
www.tile-assn.com

Tile Council of America[SM]
(864) 646-8453
www.tileusa.com

Aqua Mix
(800) 366-6877
www.aquamix.com

For a list of tile manufacturers and distributors
www.infotile.com

Hard-wearing and stain resistant. Ceramic tile, available in hundreds of colors and patterns, offers great design flexibility at a relatively low cost. But watch for grout stains.

Solid Surfacing

A 35-year-old Wunderkind in the Kitchen

Few products have had more influence in kitchen design in the past 35 years than DuPont's Corian. What was then the world's first solid-surface countertop material now has many rivals. Avonite, Gibraltar, Surell, Pionite®, Swanstone® and Fountainhead® all are brand names for essentially the same stuff: polyester or acrylic resin plus a mineral filler called ATH, or aluminum trihydrate. Solid surfacing comes in plain colors, patterns that resemble stone and, more recently, translucent versions that are glasslike in appearance.

Regardless of brand, solid surfacing has a long list of attributes that make it a nearly ideal countertop material. Solid surfacing is the same material all the way through. Minor surface blemishes—a scorch mark, for example—can be sanded out. It's nonporous, so it's easy to keep clean. And it's highly stain resistant. Solid surfacing can be fashioned into a sink and then glued to the countertop for a seamless, leakproof installation without any crevices or edges to catch and hold food and debris. It can be worked with regular woodworking tools, and solid surfacing comes with a long guarantee, usually 10 years. It's typically sold only to certified fabricators who have taken a manufacturer's training course.

Countertops are most often formed from ½-in.-thick sheets. Edges are formed by building up layers of identical or contrasting material and milling the profile with a router. Sheets 30 in. and 36 in. wide run to 12 ft. in length. Solid surfacing is expensive—roughly $50 to $100 per sq. ft.—and it's a plastic, so not as appealing to some homeowners.

Plastic that looks like stone. DuPont's Corian® revolutionized the countertop world a generation ago, and solid surfacing is still a top choice. It's now made by scores of manufacturers.

Corian

Avonite

Surell

Pros/Cons

Pros: Nonporous and nonstaining, easy to clean, repairable, durable, wide range of colors and patterns available, integral sinks possible.
Cons: High cost, should be protected from high heat, sharp knives.
Cost: Typically installed by certified fabricator, $50 to $100 per sq. ft.

Sources

Avonite
(800) 428-6648
www.avonite.com

Corian
(800) 426-7426
www.corian.com

Gibraltar
(800) 433-3222
www.wilsonart.com

Pionite
(800) 746-6483
www.pionitesolid.com

Surell, Fountainhead
(800) 367-6422
www.formica.com

Swanstone
(800) 325-7008
www.theswancorp.com

Slab Stone

Durable, Heat Resistant, and Popular

Slab stone, especially granite, is cold to the touch, heavy, hard to work, and expensive. It's also so popular, says former stone-restoration contractor Fred Hueston, that it's now going into spec houses selling for $100,000. "It's the big one now," says Hueston, owner of the National Training Center for Stone and Masonry Trades in Longwood, Florida. Granite comes from all over the world, in a variety of colors and patterns. Prices show big regional differences, starting at $40 to $50 per sq. ft. (possibly lower in some areas) and commonly running to $80 to $100 per sq. ft. installed.

Sold in two thicknesses (¾ in. and 1¼ in.), granite is resistant to heat and scratches. Most countertop material is polished, but it also is available in a honed (matte) finish, usually for a little more money. Slab size is usually limited to 10 ft. in length, 5 ft. in width.

Although resistant to acidic foods such as lemon juice, Hueston says, granite will stain. It's especially susceptible to oil. Penetrating sealers, commonly called impregnators, can keep out oil and water. Hueston prefers sealers containing fluoropolymers (the same chemical used to make Scotchgard®).

Other stone options include slate and soapstone. Both come in smaller slab sizes than granite (roughly 6 ft. long and between 30 in. and 40 in. wide) and in not nearly the variety of colors. Prices of these two types of stone are similar, $65 to $80 per sq. ft., not including installation or shipping.

Blue gray and lightly variegated when newly installed, soapstone oxidizes and darkens with time to a rich charcoal. It is extremely dense, with better stain resistance than granite. But soapstone is also soft. Soapstone is usually treated with mineral oil. Scratches in soapstone can be sanded out.

Slate runs in a wider but still limited color palette: blacks, greens, reds, grays, and muted purples. Like soapstone, slate is relatively soft, although scratch marks can be buffed out with fine steel wool, says Daphne Markcrow of Vermont Structural Slate Company in Fair Haven, Vermont. Vermont slate needs no sealers, she says, and no maintenance, although slate mined in different regions may be more absorptive. Hueston says slate, which is formed in layers, will occasionally delaminate.

Pricey but in high demand. Natural stone is the current favorite in high-end countertop choices. It offers high heat resistance and durability and a wide variety of colors and textures, such as this red-slate bar top with a honed finish.

Granite

Soapstone

Slate

Pros/Cons

Pros: Wide variety of colors and textures, heat resistant, very durable (stain and scratch resistances vary).
Cons: High cost, some types may stain, slab size may be limited. Can delaminate.
Cost: $50 to $100+ per sq. ft. fabricated and installed.

Sources

Freshwater Stone + Brickwork
(207) 469-6331
www.freshwaterstone.com

Vermont Structural Slate Co.
(800) 343-1900
www.vermontstructural slate.com

Vermont Soapstone Co.
(800) 284-5404
www.vermontsoapstone. com

Stainless Steel

The Pros Like It for a Reason

Once found only in commercial kitchens, stainless-steel counters are gaining ground at home, too. Boston architect Ann Finnerty chose a combination of stainless steel and maple butcher block when she redid her own kitchen four years ago. "I wanted a material that was common and not too precious and not too expensive," she says. Working with a local fabricator, Finnerty chose stainless steel with a plain edge and no backsplash. Finnerty likes the fact that stainless steel is easy to clean.

"When it's new especially, fingerprints show up like crazy," Finnerty says. That problem fades as the surface gets more wear and develops a patina.

Like stone and concrete countertops, stainless steel can't easily be modified on site. Countertops are usually fabricated from templates, often in 16-ga. material. Sheet metal is glued to a substrate of medium-density fiberboard. Sinks can be welded in.

Expect to pay $60 to $80 per sq. ft. But edge details, sinks and overall complexity can change prices dramatically. Mark Ponder, an estimator at Weiss Sheet Metal, which made Finnerty's counters, cautions that generalized prices can be misleading. A plain 10-ft.-long counter with a simple sink and a 4-in. backsplash might cost $1,200, he said—a price that does not include the substrate, shipping, or installation. Linda Bergling of The Stainless Steel Kitchen, a large Midwestern fabricator, says her shop charges about $160 per running foot of counter with backsplash. But the stainless is already laid up on a substrate and ready to go in.

Counters are typically made from 304 stainless with a #4 brushed finish, the same stuff used in restaurants and commercial kitchens. Length is usually limited to 10 ft., widths to 4 ft., although larger sheets can be ordered. Stainless can be cleaned with a mild detergent or baking soda or vinegar diluted in water, Bergling says, but bleach should be avoided. Some foods—including mustard, mayonnaise, lemon juice, and tomato ketchup—that sit on the counter may cause a white surface discoloration that can be rubbed out with a fine Scotch-Brite pad.

Counters also can be fashioned from copper, zinc, and nickel. But prices are usually higher, and these metals require more maintenance.

Pros/Cons

Pros: Nonporous and nonstaining, resistant to heat, durable, easy to clean.
Cons: Can dent.
Cost: $45 to $65 per sq. ft. for uninstalled straight runs; $80 to $90 installed.

Sources

The Stainless Steel Kitchen
(800) 275-1250
www.stainlesssteel
kitchen.com

GMS
(800) 787-3247

Restaurants like it. Stainless steel, long a fixture in commercial kitchens, is making gains in residential kitchens for the same reasons: long life and low maintenance.

Plastic Laminate

Old Standby Still Rules

High-pressure laminate is the family mini-van of the countertop world: It's practical and economical, and you'll never brag you own it. Still, laminate is the choice in as many as three-quarters of all new kitchens in the United States. Standard high-pressure laminate, roughly ⅟₁₆ in. thick, is a sandwich of kraft paper impregnated with phenolic resin and topped by a decorative layer of melamine-protected paper. In sheet form, laminate is glued to a particleboard substrate, either on site or in a fabricator's shop. A thinner version is manufactured into a ready-made countertop with a rounded front edge and an integral backsplash called a post-formed counter.

Laminate is available in dozens of colors and patterns for $2 or less per sq. ft. in sheets up to 12 ft. long and 5 ft. wide. Post-formed counters, ready to drop into place, may be $5 or less per sq. ft. at big home centers. There are fewer colors to choose from, and post-formed counters are for straight runs only; curvaceous kitchen designs won't work.

Most kitchen countertops are made of general-purpose laminate, but laminate is also available in high-wear, extra-thick, and fire-retardant versions. In addition to its low cost, laminate has many other attributes. Hard and durable, laminate is highly stain resistant and stands up well to everyday use. However, heat and sharp knives damage the surface, and any water getting into seams may degrade the substrate.

A variety of new edge treatments has eliminated one of laminate's long-standing aesthetic weaknesses: the dark line formed where the top of the counter meets the front edge. Edging made from wood, solid-surface material, or beveled laminate can make that seam all but invisible, but at a higher cost.

Laminate's real breakthrough in recent years has been in the top decorative layer. Digital printing and metallic inks have resulted in higher-fidelity reproduction, allowing manufacturers to create uncannily accurate patterns of materials such as wood, stone, and fabric.

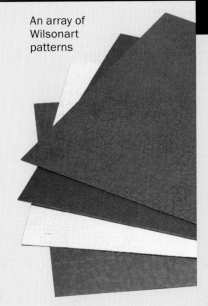
An array of Wilsonart patterns

The workhorse. Today's high-pressure laminate is aided by innovations in digital printing.

Composite Materials, Lava, and Fiber Cement

The New and the Exotic

Although many countertop materials are familiar, a variety of newer, man-made materials also is available.

Silestone is a composite of 93% quartz, resin binders and pigments. It is made in Spain and sold in the United States through a network of distributors. A similar material is made by DuPont under the Zodiaq™ brand name. Prices vary by region and by the color of the material, but installed prices are between $45 and $70 per sq. ft. It is nonporous and never needs to be sealed, the company says, and it's more resistant to food stains than the natural stone it closely resembles. Silestone is available in 35 colors and three thicknesses—$\frac{7}{16}$ in., $\frac{13}{16}$ in. and 1⅛ in.

Trespa® is a Netherlands-based company that makes three types of composite architectural panels. Two of them—TopLab™ and Athlon®—are potential kitchen countertops. Athlon is essentially super-thick high-pressure laminate. It's made from phenolic resins reinforced with cellulose fiber and manufactured under high pressure and temperature. Its top decorative layer is melamine-impregnated paper, and it is available with either a smooth or slightly textured finish. Standard sheet sizes go up to 6 ft. by 12 ft., with thicknesses ranging from ¼ in. to 1 in. One thing that makes Athlon attractive is its price: In a ½-in. thickness, Athlon is less than $7 per sq. ft. It can be worked with standard carbide tools, and it doesn't need sealing. TopLab is usually used in laboratory settings because of its resistance to chemicals, scratches, and stains. Prices are slightly higher. Pionite Sources (p. 128) makes a similar material called thick phenolic-core laminate.

In the market for something truly unusual? How about French lava with a kiln-fired enamel coating that the manufacturer says is impervious to stains and heat? Pyrolave™ comes in sheets up to 4 ft. by 8 ft., in two thicknesses—1¼ in. and 1½ in. Custom colors

Silestone quartz composite

Trespa resin composite

Zodiaq quartz composite

Fiber cement

are available in addition to the 30 stock colors the company offers. Installed prices range from $220 to $350 per sq. ft.

Fiber-cement countertops—sold under the SlateScape®, Fireslate2 and Colorlith® brand names—are manufactured in Germany, imported to the United States and sold through authorized fabricators. Fiber cement has the bulk of quarried stone, but it can be less expensive: $30 to $40 per sq. ft. in 1¼-in. thickness. Fiber cement is currently available in four colors and five thicknesses. It has good resistance to heat and has high compressive strength. Like other cement-based products, this material stains easily unless it is sealed properly—and that takes regular maintenance. The company suggests pure tung oil two or three times a year to augment the penetrating sealer applied by the fabricator.

Pyrolave

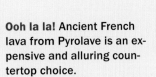

Ooh la la! Ancient French lava from Pyrolave is an expensive and alluring countertop choice.

Sources

RESIN-COMPOSITE SOURCES

Trespa North America Ltd.
(800) 487-3772
www.trespanorth america.com

FIBER-CEMENT SOURCES

American Fiber Cement Corp.
(800) 688-8677
www.americanfiber cement.com

QUARTZ-COMPOSITE SOURCES

Silestone
(800) 291-1311
www.silestoneusa.com

DuPont Zodiaq
(877) 229-3935
www.zodiaq.com

KILN-FIRED LAVA SOURCES

Pyrolave
(919) 788-8953
www.pyrolave.com

Pros/Cons

Quartz Composites
Pros: Nonporous and nonstaining, scratch and heat resistant, durable.
Cons: Relatively high cost.
Cost: $45 to $75+ per sq. ft. installed.

Resin Composites
Pros: Scratch and stain resistant, low cost.
Cons: Limited color choice, damaged by heat.
Cost: $7 to $10 per sq. ft.

Fiber Cement
Pros: Relatively low cost, heat resistant, durable, high strength.
Cons: Can stain (requires periodic resealing), limited color selection.
Cost: $30 to $70 per sq. ft. uninstalled (shipping extra).

Lava
Pros: Hard, stain resistant, heatproof.
Cons: Extremely high cost, limited availability.
Cost: $220 to $350 per sq. ft. (installed).

Ten Ways to Improve Your Kitchen

■ BY JANE K. LANGMUIR

Like others born in 1935, the average American kitchen is 65 years old and eligible for retirement. That's the date a federal task force set up during President Herbert Hoover's term in office set the standards used to design most kitchens. Hoover's aim was to pump some life into the depressed economy by putting American men to work building kitchens for American women. Standardized cabinets and appliances were at the core of the idea.

The result was the demise of the traditional unfitted kitchen, in which individual pieces of furniture comprised a kitchen's storage space and work surfaces. In its place, the fitted kitchen emerged, with its linear runs of built-in base and wall cabinets separating the triangle of sink, stove and refrigerator. For 50 years, the only things that changed were colors, trim styles, and materials. But there are signs that that era is over.

The kitchen is now the most-used room in the home. It is everyone's domain. It is the

A gathering space amid the action.
Surrounded by counters of different heights, this kitchen has a breakfast table at its heart. On the far wall, a long, shallow prep sink is topped by a slatted pot rack.

place for nurturing body, mind and soul. It is communication and food central—ground zero for planning and scheduling, the center for social contact and information, and last but certainly not least, the workplace with the engines that prepare our meals.

Beginning in 1993, I directed a five-year study at the Rhode Island School of Design that eventually included more than 100 students and faculty members. Our goal was to identify the reasons that kitchens are typically bastions of poor design. All too often, our kitchens make us bend, stoop, retrace our steps, and work in poor light at counters that are too high or too low. Based on what we learned in our studies and on the lessons I've learned as a designer, I offer these 10 ways to help move your kitchen into the 21st century.

1. Consider the Comfort Zone

For a kitchen to be your own, it has to fit your comfort zone. What's a comfort zone? It is the space defined by the comfortable reach between one hand raised above your head and the other dropped to your side (drawing, below). This range applies to both sitting and standing; the key is that everybody has a different comfort zone. This means you should adjust a kitchen's components to fit its primary user. To that end, start by:

- Getting rid of upper cabinets, or pulling out the counter a bit and bringing the cabinets down to counter level (photo, p. 137).

Store Kitchen Supplies in the Comfort Zone

The comfort zone is the space defined by the comfortable reach between one hand raised above your head and the other dropped to your side. Use these measurements to locate storage areas for your most-frequently needed supplies and utensils.

Comfort zones apply to both sitting and standing.

Find the Counter Height That's Right for You

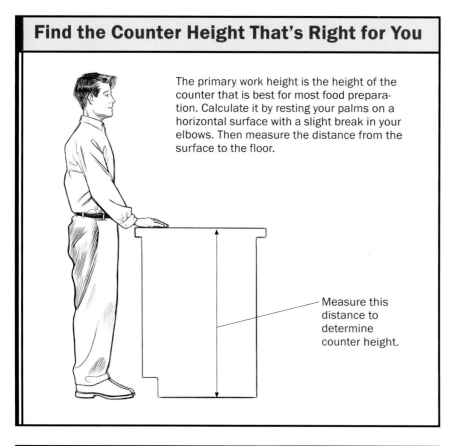

The primary work height is the height of the counter that is best for most food preparation. Calculate it by resting your palms on a horizontal surface with a slight break in your elbows. Then measure the distance from the surface to the floor.

Measure this distance to determine counter height.

Optimum Work Zone

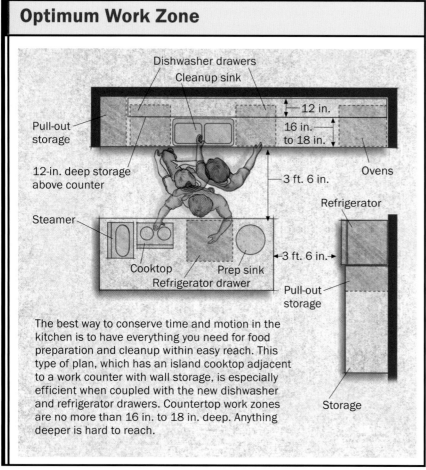

Dishwasher drawers
Cleanup sink
Pull-out storage
12-in. deep storage above counter
Steamer
Cooktop
Refrigerator drawer
Prep sink
12 in.
16 in. to 18 in.
Ovens
3 ft. 6 in.
Refrigerator
3 ft. 6 in.
Pull-out storage
Storage

The best way to conserve time and motion in the kitchen is to have everything you need for food preparation and cleanup within easy reach. This type of plan, which has an island cooktop adjacent to a work counter with wall storage, is especially efficient when coupled with the new dishwasher and refrigerator drawers. Countertop work zones are no more than 16 in. to 18 in. deep. Anything deeper is hard to reach.

- Storing less-essential tools, dishes, cookware, and foodstuffs in tall, pull-out storage units or in pantries away from work zones. Everybody can find their comfort-zone range within either of these storage options.

2. Who Needs a 36-in. High Counter?

The standards set back in the '30s called for a 36-in. counter height. It was set to meet the ergonomic needs of the average homemaker. She was 5 ft. 4 in. to 5 ft. 5 in. tall and fully able. Today, we are designing for a much broader population range, and we need to acknowledge that everyone's needs are different. In fact, each person should have a minimum of three different counter heights for performing kitchen tasks.

First, you want to establish the primary counter height by resting the palms of your hands on a horizontal surface with a slight break in your elbows (top drawing). Next, have someone measure the distance from the floor to the surface. This counter height is best for most prepping.

At the sink, the height of the counter should ideally be 3 in. to 5 in. higher depending on the depth of the sink. For cooking, the counter height should be 2 in. or 3 in. lower so that you can easily see in the cooking pots and so that you can have increased reach with a utensil in hand.

3. Shrink the Kitchen Triangle

The triangle has been the basis for organizing the kitchen footprint since the beginning of fitted kitchens. The theory is that the work areas should be inside a triangle that connects the refrigerator, sink, and stove. This arrangement supposedly yields the most efficient work flow. But over time, this triangle connection has been undermined as kitchens have grown. Contemporary kitchens often have more counter space between the three points of the triangle. An island in the center of the kitchen will further impede traffic between the stove, the sink, and the refrigerator.

We conducted time and motion studies in our kitchen project and concluded that you can reduce by half the time taken to prepare a simple meal by eliminating unnecessary walking. The way to do this is to make sure you have the essential elements for preparing a meal within reach of your work zone. Frequently used foods and condiments, water, utensils, pots, pans, and a cooktop should all be within reach. A good layout for a kitchen is an island backed up by a work and storage wall (bottom drawing, facing page).

4. Water, Water Everywhere

There is not one task in the kitchen that doesn't require water. So isn't it odd that there is usually only one sink or water source in a kitchen? For food preparation, I prefer a long, troughlike sink that isn't too deep—4 in. to 5 in. at the most. I don't know of any commercially available sinks like this. We had the one shown here fabricated by a local metal shop out of stainless steel (bottom photo).

Keep in mind the cleanup sink should not be used as a holding dishwasher. Instead, consider the dishwasher as a holding sink. This usage frees the sink, or sinks, for prepping and cleaning, ready for the next task.

5. A Cart Offers Flexibility

A cart with a work surface can serve several functions in the kitchen. It can act as a ferry between two work surfaces, allowing for easy conveyance of hot, heavy pots. It can become an additional work surface when necessary. More elaborate versions can be

Put essentials within easy reach. Bringing the upper cabinets down to counter height makes it easy to grab frequently needed supplies. As a bonus, lowering the upper cabinets makes room for a row of windows. Open shelves below the cooktop provide ready access to pots and pans.

A flexible prep sink. Long and shallow, this custom-made stainless-steel sink is designed specifically for preparing food. Generous drain boards and a pair of chopping blocks make additional work surfaces.

Carts provide storage and work surface. A rolling workstation such as this one can expand counter space as needed or act as a truck to ferry heavy, hot pots from one part of the kitchen to another. This cart is outfitted with trash bins on heavy-duty drawer pulls at each end.

Pots and pans at the ready. Above the prep sink, a pot rack is purposefully positioned to let freshly washed cookware drain harmlessly into the sink. Pans rest on teak slats in their own cubby holes.

made with adjustable-height work surfaces, or even refrigeration or cooking capabilities.

The cart shown at left serves yet another function: It has twin trash receptacles that ride on heavy-duty drawer slides. And trash/recycling/composting space in the kitchen is right up there with water in importance. When not in use, the cart should slip under a counter out of the way.

6. Watch Out for the Doors

It would be a great boon in the kitchen if doors could disappear at the click of a switch or on the command of a voice. Alas, we are not there yet. However, there are solutions to get rid of the knee and shin bangers.

- If at all possible, don't place the oven below the counter. A wall oven within your comfort zone is much better.

- Raise the dishwasher 6 in. to 10 in. off the floor. This placement will save your shins and a lot of unnecessary bending. Or install a dish drawer.

- Eliminate all door-and-drawer combinations. You will save the doors from getting banged around and also the time it takes to accomplish two operations. Whenever possible, a drawer below counter height is a better option than a cabinet shelf.

7. Appliances That Make It Work

There are several great appliances that have been introduced to the marketplace in the past few years that make working in the kitchen a dream. They are still a bit pricey, but if you can afford them, they're worth it. And as they gain acceptance, competition will likely force down prices.

- Sub-Zero®'s 700 series refrigerator drawers can be placed under the counter in your work zone, bringing fresh produce to the task at hand (top photo).

- Fisher-Paykel's drawer dishwashers can be placed under the counter in the prep or cleanup zone. They provide easy, visible access with no bending or shin-cracking doors, and they are great as holding sinks until you are ready to run a cycle of dishes (bottom left photo).

- Two-burner cooktops and individual grills and griddles (photo, p. 140), such as General Electric®'s Monogram® series and Maytag®'s Expressions Collection series, have several advantages over conventional cooktops. First, you can turn the units 90° so that you don't have to reach over hot burners. Second, you can select different fuel options, such as a high-Btu gas burner for wok cooking or an electric burner for boiling water. And third, you have the option of placing different units for different tasks wherever you like.

- Another modular appliance that can add convenience to your kitchen in Gaggenau®'s VK 111 built-in steamer (bottom right photo). At approximately 20 in. by 12 in., the unit takes up little space. You can cook a variety of foods in it, from rice to fish to vegetables. And it can be hooked up to a drain line for easy cleanup.

8. Use Materials That Combine Beauty and Durability

There are a number of interesting new materials flooding the marketplace, but none can beat the inherent qualities of natural materials for their efficiency, durability, sustainability, and beauty.

Pullout fridge. Sub-Zero's refrigerator drawers let you strategically place fresh foods near kitchen work zones.

A drawer full of dirty dishes will get clean if they're in Fisher-Paykel's dishwasher drawer.

A built-in steamer that's easy to clean. Mounted in a counter, Gaggenau's electric steamer expands a cook's options and frees up cooktop space. The steamer can be hooked up to a drain for easy cleanup.

A cooking wall. Modular burners can be arranged in the traditional front/back relationship, or turned sideways to make a cooktop that is one burner deep.

Wood is excellent for all surfaces: counters, cabinet doors and drawers, and floors. Whether painted or left natural, it brings warmth and color. Wood can easily be refurbished, lasting a lifetime.

Stainless steel, as a countertop material, is easy to clean and nonporous, withstands hot and cold, and lasts a lifetime.

Glass panels in cabinet doors are a delight in a kitchen, especially if the cabinets include glass shelves and are lighted from within. Either transparent or translucent glass does the trick. You can see where things are, and especially in small dark places, the transparency creates lightness and brightness.

Stone makes a great counter, bringing warmth and personal color choice. One caution: It can discolor and hold stains.

Tile, whether ceramic or stone, will add color and durability to a kitchen. But try to avoid it on horizontal work surfaces, where its grout joints are hard to keep clean. Tile is best used as a backsplash or wall finish behind a sink or a stove.

9. Good Kitchens Need Good Lighting

If they have not been recently remodeled, most kitchens suffer from bad lighting. The common kitchen-lighting scheme is one light in the center of the ceiling and maybe a light over the sink. That's not enough. There should be three types of lighting in the kitchen:

- General ceiling lighting provides light for passage and overall clarity.

- Task lighting over counter or under upper cabinets highlights specific work zones.

- Mood lighting changes the kitchen from a workplace to a place for meals from simple suppers to fine dining or a social gathering.

These uses can all be achieved by recessed lights or by a combination of recessed, surface-mount, pendant, cable or track lighting. Each type of lighting should be switched separately with light levels controlled by dimmer switches.

10. The Kitchen Window Isn't What It Used to Be

A window centered over the kitchen sink is fine, but it isn't the driving design force that it once was. The new window view is the kitchen itself and all that is going on: the kids eating or playing, friends or family helping, guests relaxing, or just enjoying the layers of light and complexity from the other windows within sight. Use this concept to create places within the kitchen that people want to occupy.

Jane K. Langmuir is a principal partner in Jane K. Langmuir, Inc. and has taught at the Rhode Island School of Design in Providence, Rhode Island.

Getting Appliances to Fit

■ BY DAVID GETTS

A few years ago, I got a call from a customer who wanted me to know that the electronics in her wall oven had burned out. I had installed the appliance only a year earlier, just long enough for the warranty to run out, and the news from the repairman who soon visited the house wasn't much better. He suggested they call me because the problem was my fault. According to the company, I had failed to drill vent holes in the oven cabinet to prevent overheating. As soon as the customers started the self-cleaning cycle, the delicate circuitry was, well, toast.

I knew I had saved the installation instructions, and when I went back to check them, I found nothing about adding ventilation to the cabinet. Not a word. Shown their own installation specs, the manufacturer agreed to cover the cost of repair as well as my time for modifying the oven cabinet. If the experience proved anything, it's that even following the manufacturer's instructions to the letter is no guarantee that an appliance installation will go smoothly. But it sure improves your odds.

These days, I insist clients choose their appliances before kitchen-design work starts. I make sure I have the most recent installation guides from the manufacturer (or I check www.dexpress.com for current dimensions). Remembering the hard-learned tricks presented here doesn't hurt, either.

David Getts is a cabinetmaker in Bothell, Washington.

Under-Counter Built-in Oven

Ovens generate a lot of heat (as I learned), so great care should be taken to follow the manufacturer's instructions on minimum clearances. Overheating can damage the oven or, worse, cause a fire. The distance between the side of the oven and cabinet is critical. In a frameless cabinet, an extra cabinet side or a filler strip may be needed to keep the oven at least 1 in. away from Thermofoil doors, which can be damaged by high heat. Some cabinet manufacturers provide an extra cabinet box for the oven, which provides this extra clearance, or you can add your own to adjacent cabinet sides.

FRAMELESS CABINETS

Check manufacturer's recommended clearance between oven and cabinet, typically ½ in. to 1 in.

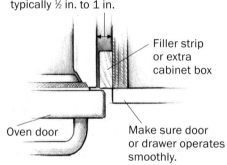

Filler strip or extra cabinet box

Oven door

Make sure door or drawer operates smoothly.

FACE-FRAME CABINETS

Check clearance between oven and cabinet side.

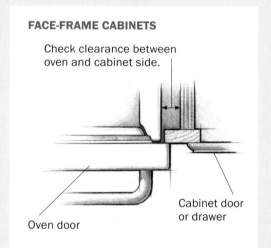

Oven door

Cabinet door or drawer

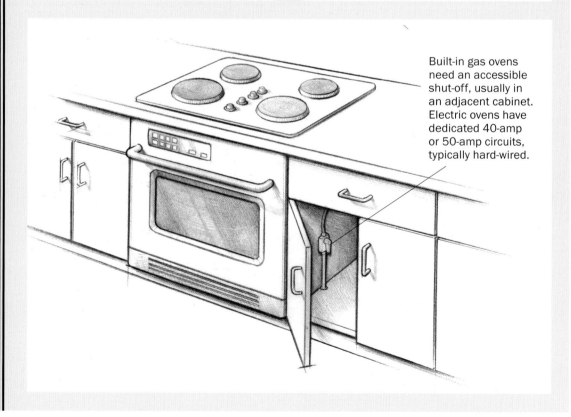

Built-in gas ovens need an accessible shut-off, usually in an adjacent cabinet. Electric ovens have dedicated 40-amp or 50-amp circuits, typically hard-wired.

Built-in Microwave

Although microwave ovens often are mounted over the cooktop where they double as a vent hood, they sometimes are installed in a cabinet. Because there is no ductwork, a built-in requires nothing more than a 110v outlet and a properly sized cabinet. Remember to follow the manufacturer's cabinet-size requirements closely so that the trim kit, if there is one, fits accurately. The single most important consideration is installation height. In one installation I did, the owner insisted on a certain height above the countertop even though I thought it was too high. They won the argument. Even with my 6-ft. frame, I couldn't see the inside bottom of the microwave standing on my toes. Both husband and wife were tall, but the location would make that microwave awkward for anyone else to use.

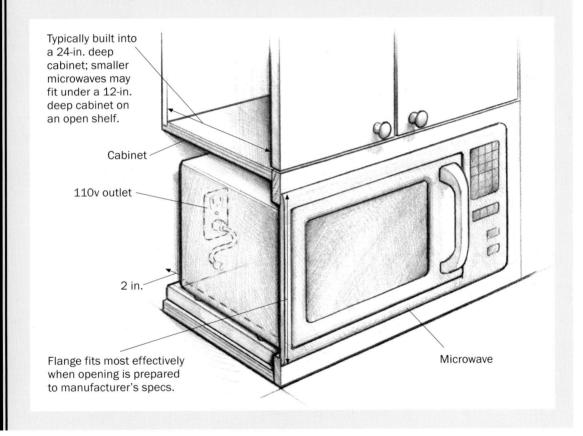

Typically built into a 24-in. deep cabinet; smaller microwaves may fit under a 12-in. deep cabinet on an open shelf.

Cabinet

110v outlet

2 in.

Flange fits most effectively when opening is prepared to manufacturer's specs.

Microwave

Oven-Cooktop Microwave

Microwave ovens mounted over the cooktop have become extremely popular in recent years. Functioning as both a microwave and a stove vent, these appliances save both space and money. Because they are designed to fit in a 30-in.-wide opening (the same as a standard cooktop), they can replace an old vent hood or over-the-stove cabinet in a retrofit. Many can be set up to vent to the outside or to recirculate air through filters. Vent pipe is typically 7-in. dia. with a 3¼-in. by 10-in. transition where it connects to the appliance. Microwaves come with a pigtail attachment to plug into a 110v outlet (20-amp dedicated circuit) that should be located in the cabinet above.

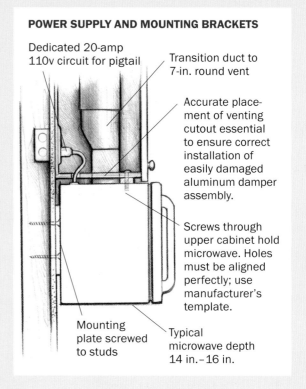

POWER SUPPLY AND MOUNTING BRACKETS

Dedicated 20-amp 110v circuit for pigtail

Transition duct to 7-in. round vent

Accurate placement of venting cutout essential to ensure correct installation of easily damaged aluminum damper assembly.

Screws through upper cabinet hold microwave. Holes must be aligned perfectly; use manufacturer's template.

Mounting plate screwed to studs

Typical microwave depth 14 in.–16 in.

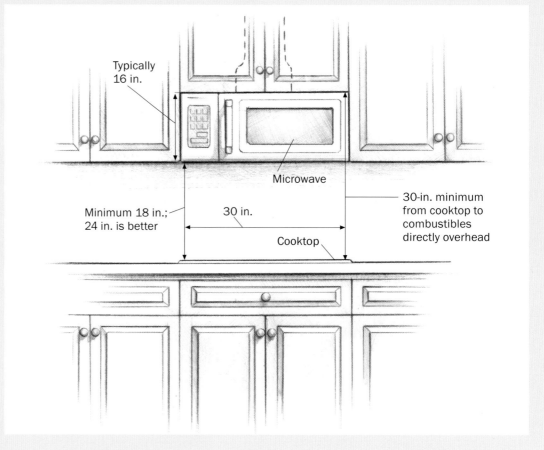

Typically 16 in.

Microwave

Minimum 18 in.; 24 in. is better

30 in.

30-in. minimum from cooktop to combustibles directly overhead

Cooktop

Drop-in Cooktop

Drop-in cooktops are the way to go for a sleek look. As the name implies, these appliances are dropped into a cutout in the countertop, much like a self-rimming sink. One advantage is that the front edge of the countertop and the cabinets below are continuous for a cleaner look. Another is that there are no spaces for food to fall into. Using a separate cooktop also expands the options for an oven, which is installed separately and can be from a different manufacturer. Knowing the exact depth of the cooktop is critical so that cabinets below can be designed correctly; cooktops usually are no more than 4 in. deep, allowing the use of a shallow drawer directly below the cooktop.

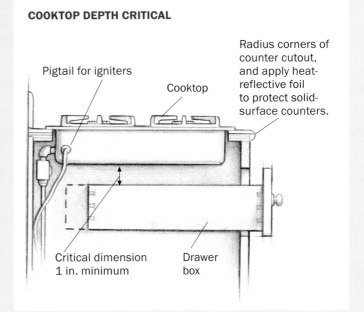

COOKTOP DEPTH CRITICAL

Pigtail for igniters

Cooktop

Radius corners of counter cutout, and apply heat-reflective foil to protect solid-surface counters.

Critical dimension 1 in. minimum

Drawer box

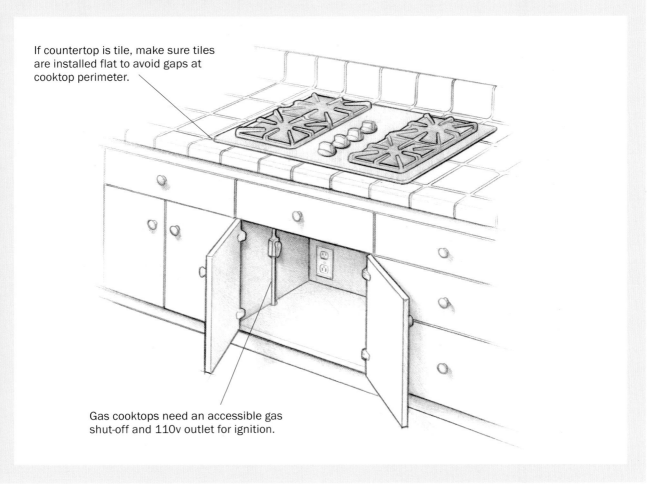

If countertop is tile, make sure tiles are installed flat to avoid gaps at cooktop perimeter.

Gas cooktops need an accessible gas shut-off and 110v outlet for ignition.

Downdraft Ventilation

Downdraft venting systems are mounted on the cooktop surface, either as a separate unit or as an integral part of the cooktop or range. As the name implies, these units vent through the floor. If you are installing a cooktop with a downdraft feature, pay close attention to the manufacturer's specifications. These units often have tight tolerances, and you want to be sure that cabinets can accommodate ducts and the blower motor. Slide-in ranges with an attached downdraft unit usually have a flange duct plate that mounts to the floor for easy installation. As with overhead venting options, the key is to avoid floor or ceiling joists, and to make ducting as straight as possible. Cabinet dimensions are critical. If the downdraft unit is made by a different manufacturer than the cooktop or the range, check compatibility.

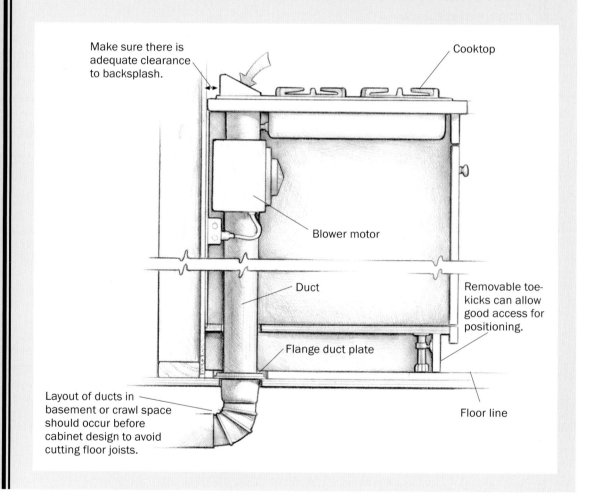

Make sure there is adequate clearance to backsplash.

Cooktop

Blower motor

Duct

Removable toe-kicks can allow good access for positioning.

Flange duct plate

Floor line

Layout of ducts in basement or crawl space should occur before cabinet design to avoid cutting floor joists.

Updraft Ventilation

Updraft vents installed on a wall above the cooktop or stove—typically beneath an upper cabinet—are vented to the outside either through a sidewall or through the roof. They are relatively simple to install. These units are hard-wired from the back and vented through the top. Four screws attach the hood to the cabinet above. Upgraded versions enclose the hood in a wood, tile, or stone shroud. Although an added shroud makes for a more difficult installation, the mechanics are the same. Wide hoods over the stove, those 24 in. deep, should be installed slightly higher than a standard hood—30 in. to 36 in. instead of 24 in. to 30 in. That's also the rule for commercial-style installations. The other type of updraft ventilation is a hood that hangs from the ceiling, usually over a kitchen island. My biggest concern here is to make sure the unit is securely fastened to the ceiling, so adequate blocking in the ceiling is essential. It also can be a challenge to locate the hood so that it will be centered over the island. Both types of vent systems require careful layout to avoid floor and ceiling joists. When ducting, use as straight a run as possible.

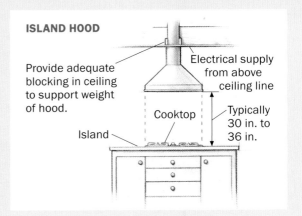

ISLAND HOOD

Provide adequate blocking in ceiling to support weight of hood.

Electrical supply from above ceiling line

Cooktop

Island

Typically 30 in. to 36 in.

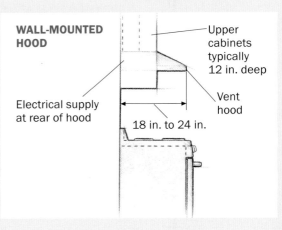

WALL-MOUNTED HOOD

Upper cabinets typically 12 in. deep

Electrical supply at rear of hood

Vent hood

18 in. to 24 in.

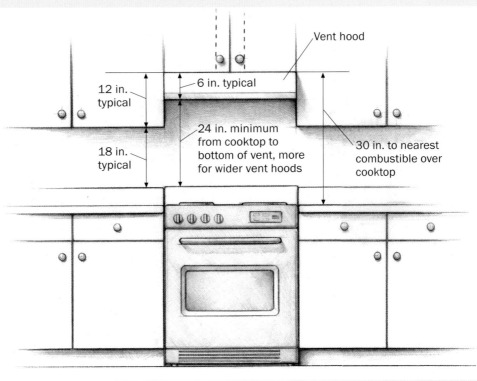

Vent hood

12 in. typical

6 in. typical

18 in. typical

24 in. minimum from cooktop to bottom of vent, more for wider vent hoods

30 in. to nearest combustible over cooktop

Free-Standing and Slide-in Ranges

ree-standing and slide-in ranges are most common. Although installation is essentially the same, there are some differences worth noting. Free-standing appliances have two finished ends and are independent of the cabinets and countertop. A free-standing range stands slightly taller than the countertop, and there is a small gap between the appliance and the edge of the countertop. Slide-in ranges are similar in appearance except that the top has a trim flange that overlaps the countertop cutout. They appear built-in. Installation requires leveling the appliance until the trim flange comes in contact with the countertop surface. They both combine a cooktop with an oven in a single metal cabinet. Most measure 30 in. wide (some are 27 in.) and require an opening of 30 in.

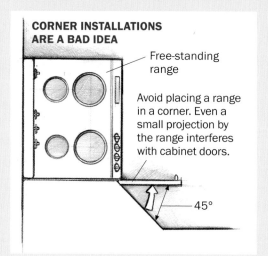

CORNER INSTALLATIONS ARE A BAD IDEA

Free-standing range

Avoid placing a range in a corner. Even a small projection by the range interferes with cabinet doors.

45°

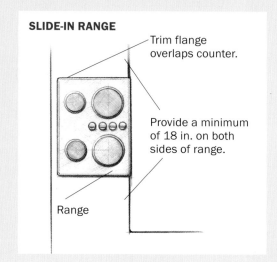

SLIDE-IN RANGE

Trim flange overlaps counter.

Provide a minimum of 18 in. on both sides of range.

Range

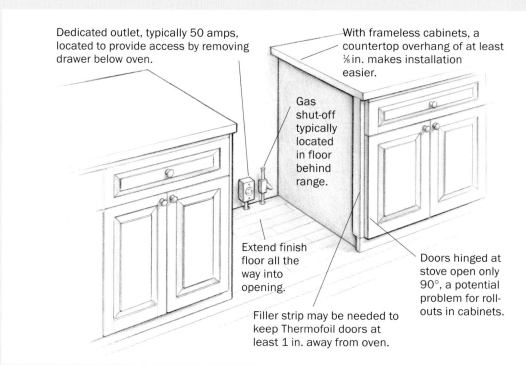

Dedicated outlet, typically 50 amps, located to provide access by removing drawer below oven.

With frameless cabinets, a countertop overhang of at least ⅛ in. makes installation easier.

Gas shut-off typically located in floor behind range.

Extend finish floor all the way into opening.

Filler strip may be needed to keep Thermofoil doors at least 1 in. away from oven.

Doors hinged at stove open only 90°, a potential problem for roll-outs in cabinets.

Refrigerators

The refrigerator is the largest appliance in the kitchen. Standard slide-in refrigerators require no special allowances other than providing a hole big enough to get it in and out—usually a hole 1 in. wider than the refrigerator is enough. Height allowances can be more generous: By allowing 2 in. to 3 in. from the top of the appliance to the bottom of the cabinet, you give the refrigerator a little breathing room and make installation easier. This gap is concealed with a filler strip. If floors are not level, it's helpful to have extra room so that the refrigerator can be leveled. Depths are typically 27 in. to 32 in., making the appliance project from the cabinet face by up to 8 in. If this is undesirable, a built-in refrigerator such as the Sub-Zero is a good choice. Their overall depth is 24 in., although they are generally taller than a standard model. The only mechanical considerations to keep in mind are the 110v outlet (on a dedicated circuit) and a cold-water line for the ice maker if the refrigerator has one.

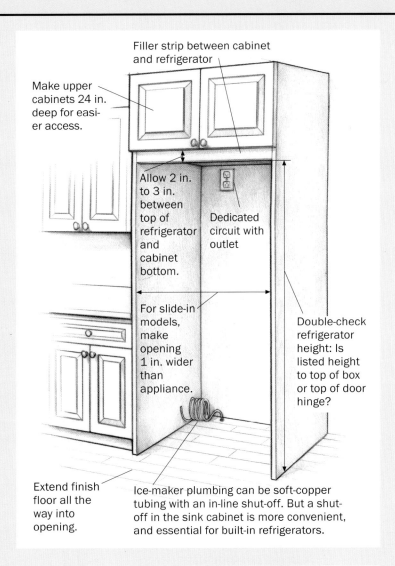

Filler strip between cabinet and refrigerator

Make upper cabinets 24 in. deep for easier access.

Allow 2 in. to 3 in. between top of refrigerator and cabinet bottom.

Dedicated circuit with outlet

For slide-in models, make opening 1 in. wider than appliance.

Double-check refrigerator height: Is listed height to top of box or top of door hinge?

Extend finish floor all the way into opening.

Ice-maker plumbing can be soft-copper tubing with an in-line shut-off. But a shut-off in the sink cabinet is more convenient, and essential for built-in refrigerators.

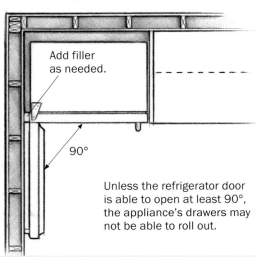

IN A CORNER, MAKE SURE THE DOOR OPENS

Add filler as needed.

90°

Unless the refrigerator door is able to open at least 90°, the appliance's drawers may not be able to roll out.

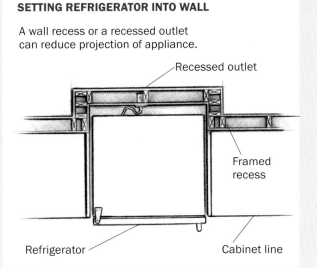

SETTING REFRIGERATOR INTO WALL

A wall recess or a recessed outlet can reduce projection of appliance.

Recessed outlet

Framed recess

Refrigerator

Cabinet line

Wall Ovens

Wall ovens are designed for a built-in look, and they provide flexibility in kitchen design because they don't have to be located under the cooktop. This freedom is especially helpful when raising the oven off the floor for a more comfortable working height (between 18 in. and 30 in. is typical) or when the cook needs two ovens. Trim around the oven perimeter overlaps the front of the cabinet. In frame-less cabinets, a separate frame may be needed so that the oven flange does not interfere with adjacent cabinets. The most critical issue is air circulation. Most wall ovens have a vent that allows hot air to escape from the front of the appliance, but some manufacturers require an additional vent hole in the back of the cabinet floor to aid in ventilation.

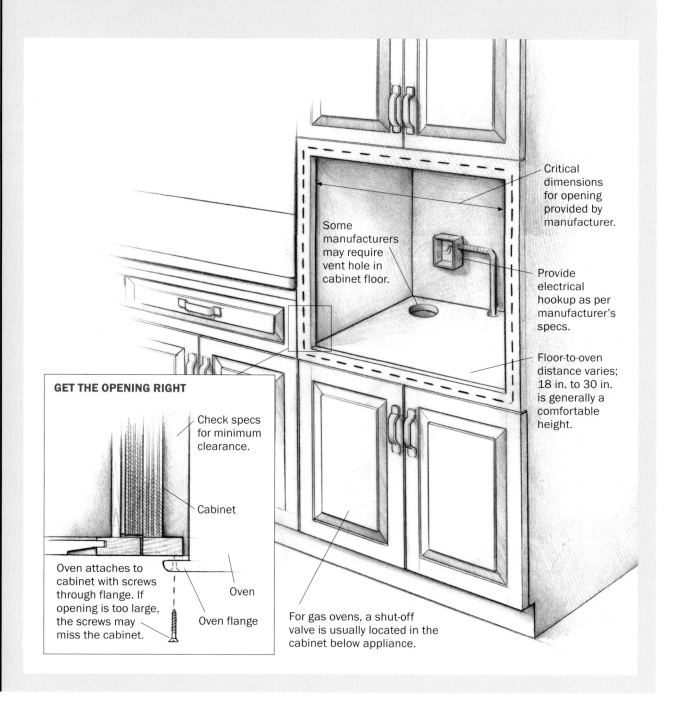

Some manufacturers may require vent hole in cabinet floor.

Critical dimensions for opening provided by manufacturer.

Provide electrical hookup as per manufacturer's specs.

Floor-to-oven distance varies; 18 in. to 30 in. is generally a comfortable height.

GET THE OPENING RIGHT

Check specs for minimum clearance.

Cabinet

Oven attaches to cabinet with screws through flange. If opening is too large, the screws may miss the cabinet.

Oven

Oven flange

For gas ovens, a shut-off valve is usually located in the cabinet below appliance.

Dishwashers

For years, dishwasher openings were always 24 in. wide. Now that many dishwashers are imported from Europe, that's no longer the case. European models typically require a 23⅝-in. opening. Another key consideration is the dishwasher's proximity to the kitchen sink. Most dishwashers are installed next to the sink cabinet (it should not be more than 5 ft. away) to allow for easy access to the plumbing. Hot water should have its own shut-off valve with ⅜-in. soft-copper or braided-steel line running to the appliance. Waste water is carried by a ⅝-in. flexible rubber or plastic hose to the sink waste line. A dedicated 110v circuit is required. Most jurisdictions in my area allow dishwashers to be hard-wired, but I know of one city nearby that requires an outlet and a pigtail. It's a good idea to check that point with the local building inspector. By the way, you can eliminate the sink-mounted air gap with a wall-mounted version called a Johnson T (Johnson Industries℠; 800-548-6895).

BE WARY OF CORNER INSTALLATIONS

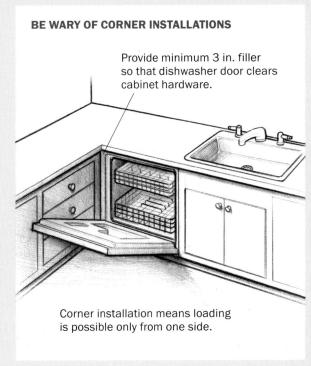

Provide minimum 3 in. filler so that dishwasher door clears cabinet hardware.

Corner installation means loading is possible only from one side.

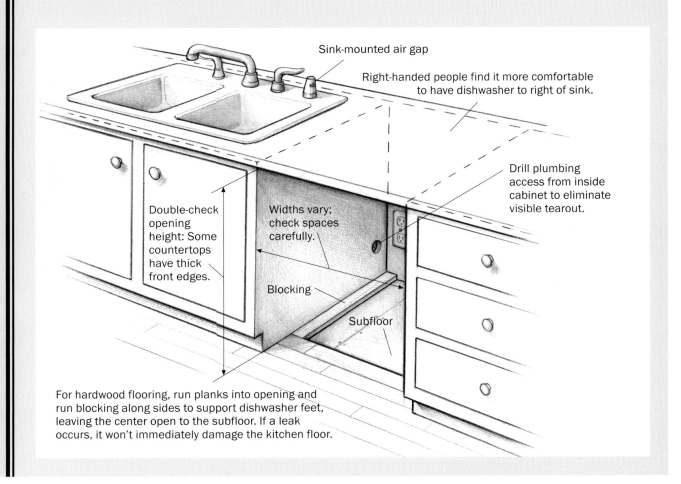

Sink-mounted air gap

Right-handed people find it more comfortable to have dishwasher to right of sink.

Double-check opening height: Some countertops have thick front edges.

Widths vary; check spaces carefully.

Drill plumbing access from inside cabinet to eliminate visible tearout.

Blocking

Subfloor

For hardwood flooring, run planks into opening and run blocking along sides to support dishwasher feet, leaving the center open to the subfloor. If a leak occurs, it won't immediately damage the kitchen floor.

CREDITS

The articles compiled in this book appeared in the following issues of *Fine Homebuilding*:

Table of contents: Photos on p. iv (left) © Robert Reck; p. iv (right) by Charles Miller, courtesy of *Fine Homebuilding*, © The Taunton Press, Inc.; p. v (left) by Scott Gibson, courtesy of *Fine Homebuilding*, © The Taunton Press, Inc.; p. v (right) by Roe A. Osborn, courtesy of *Fine Homebuilding*, © The Taunton Press, Inc.

p. 4: Kitchen Cabinets from Components by Joel Wheeler and Sven Hanson, issue 91. Photos on p. 4 © Robert Reck; pp. 6–11 © Sven Hanson.

p. 13: Hybrid Cabinet Construction by Jim Tolpin, issue 74. Photos on pp. 13, 15, and 19 (bottom) by Bruce Greenlaw, courtesy of *Fine Homebuilding*, © The Taunton Press, Inc.; pp. 17, 18, and 19 (top) by Patrick Cudahy, courtesy of *Fine Homebuilding*, © The Taunton Press, Inc. Illustrations by Bob Goodfellow, © The Taunton Press, Inc.

p. 21: Installing Kitchen Cabinets by Tom Law, issue 85. Photos by Rich Ziegner, courtesy of *Fine Homebuilding*, © The Taunton Press, Inc. Illustrations, © Christopher Clapp.

p. 34: Building Kitchen Cabinets on Site by Joseph B. Lanza, issue 126. Photos by Scott Gibson, courtesy of *Fine Homebuilding*, © The Taunton Press, Inc.

p. 42: Faux Fridge Front by Mike Guertin, issue 127. Photos by Roe A. Osborn, courtesy of *Fine Homebuilding*, © The Taunton Press, Inc. Illustration by Paul Perreault, © The Taunton Press, Inc.

p. 45: Installing Kitchen Cabinets by Kevin Luddy, issue 132. Photos by Roe A. Osborn, courtesy of *Fine Homebuilding*, © The Taunton Press, Inc.

p. 54: Simple Frameless Cabinets Built on Site, by Joseph B. Lanza, issue 138. Photos by Scott Gibson, courtesy of *Fine Homebuilding*, © The Taunton Press, Inc. Illustration by Dan Thornton, © The Taunton Press, Inc.

p. 60: Making a Solid-Surface Countertop by Sven Hanson, issue 84. Photos on pp. 61, 63–66 (top), and 67–70 by Charles Miller, courtesy of *Fine Homebuilding*, © The Taunton Press, Inc.; pp. 66 (bottom) and 71 © Sven Hanson. Illustrations © Maria Meleschnig.

p. 72: Making Concrete Countertops by Thomas Hughes, issue 90. Photos on p. 73 by Charles Miller, courtesy of *Fine Homebuilding*, © The Taunton Press, Inc.; pp. 74–77 © Thomas Hughes.

p. 78: Making Plastic-Laminate Countertops by Herrick Kimball, issue 75. Photos by Kevin Ireton, courtesy of *Fine Homebuilding*, © The Taunton Press, Inc.

p. 89: Counter Act by Steve Morris, issue 121. Photos by Zachary Gaulkin, courtesy of *Fine Homebuilding*, © The Taunton Press, Inc.

p. 97: Tiling a Kitchen Counter by Dennis Hourany, issue 120. Photos by Scott Gibson, courtesy of *Fine Homebuilding*, © The Taunton Press, Inc. Illustrations by Dan Thornton, © The Taunton Press, Inc.

p. 109: Tiling over a Laminate Counter by David Hart, issue 130. Photos by Charles Bickford, courtesy of *Fine Homebuilding*, © The Taunton Press, Inc.

p. 114: An Inside Look at Kitchen Cabinets by Scott Gibson, issue 127. Photos on p. 114 by Scott Gibson, courtesy of *Fine Homebuilding*, © The Taunton Press, Inc.; pp. 117–119, 121–123 by Scott Phillips, courtesy of *Fine Homebuilding*, © The Taunton Press, Inc.

p. 124: Choosing Kitchen Countertops by Scott Gibson, issue 143. Photos on p. 124 by Andy Engel, courtesy of *Fine Homebuilding,* © The Taunton Press, Inc.; pp. 125, 126 (top), 127 (top), 128 (bottom), 129 (top), 130 (top), 131, 132 and 133 (top) by Scott Phillips, courtesy of *Fine Homebuilding,* © The Taunton Press, Inc.; p. 126 (bottom) by Charles Miller, courtesy of *Fine Homebuilding,* © The Taunton Press, Inc.; p. 127 (bottom) by Roe A. Osborn, courtesy of *Fine Homebuilding,* © The Taunton Press, Inc.; p. 128 (top) courtesy of DuPont; p. 129 (bottom) courtesy Vermont Structural Slate Co.; p. 130 (bottom) by Claudio Santini; p. 133 (bottom) courtesy of Pyrolave.

p. 134: Ten Ways to Improve Your Kitchen by Jane K. Langmuir, issue 135. Photos on pp. 134, 137, 138 (bottom), 139, 140 by Charles Miller, courtesy of *Fine Homebuilding,* © The Taunton Press, Inc.; p. 138 (top) by Aaron Pennock; Illustrations by Matt Collins, © The Taunton Press, Inc.

p. 141: Getting Appliances to Fit by David Getts, issue 143. Illustrations by Bob La Pointe, © The Taunton Press, Inc.

INDEX